TENNIS TACTICS

Winning Patterns of Play

United States Tennis Association

Human Kinetics

Library of Congress Cataloging-in-Publication Data

Tennis tactics : winning patterns of play / United States Tennis
  Association.
       p.   cm.
    ISBN 0-88011-499-1
    1. Tennis--Training.   2. Tennis--Singles.   I. United States
Tennis Association
    GV1002.9.T7T45   1996
    796.342'07--dc20   96-21957
                                                                 CIP

ISBN: 0-88011-499-1

Developmental Editor: Rodd Whelpley; **Assistant Editor:** Kent Reel; **Editorial
Assistant:** Jennifer Hemphill; **Copyeditor:** Barbara Field; **Proofreader:** Bob
Replinger; **Text Designer:** Judy Henderson; **Layout Artist:** Tara Welsch; **Photo
Editor:** Boyd La Foon; **Cover Designer:** Keith Blomberg; **Photographer (cover):**
Cynthia Lum; **Photographers (interior):** Pages 1, 19, 105, 143, Russ Adams; page
185, Lance Jeffrey; **Illustrator:** Jennifer Delmotte; **Printer:** United Graphics

Human Kinetics books are available at special discounts for bulk purchase.
Special editions or book excerpts can also be created to specification. For details,
contact the Special Sales Manager at Human Kinetics.

Printed in the United States of America   10 9 8 7 6 5 4 3 2 1

Human Kinetics
Web site: http://www.humankinetics.com/

United States: Human Kinetics, P.O. Box 5076, Champaign, IL 61825-5076
1-800-747-4457
e-mail: humank@hkusa.com

Canada: Human Kinetics, Box 24040, Windsor, ON N8Y 4Y9
1-800-465-7301 (in Canada only)
e-mail: humank@hkcanada.com

Europe: Human Kinetics, P.O. Box IW14, Leeds LS16 6TR, United Kingdom
(44) 1132 781708
e-mail: humank@hkeurope.com

Australia: Human Kinetics, 57A Price Avenue
Lower Mitcham, South Australia 5062
(08) 277 1555
e-mail: humank@hkaustralia.com

New Zealand: Human Kinetics, P.O. Box 105-231, Auckland 1
(09) 523 3462
e-mail: humank@hknewz.com

Contents

Foreword

"Tennis is becoming too much of a power game!"

"Too few rallies and too many short points—it's not at all like the game was meant to be played."

Statements like these reflect a lack of knowledge about the game—or, at least, too narrow a focus on the strongest-serving professional players in men's tennis. The fact is that tennis is still the great sport it has been, but it requires that those who wish to play it well develop a whole set of attributes and build on them.

Conditioning, first among these attributes, is a must. Strength, power, quickness, agility, and endurance are essential physical tools for any serious player.

Second, a competitive mind-set is necessary for playing great tennis. I know from personal experience that when the fire for the game is not in my belly, my game suffers accordingly. Conversely, when the competitive fires burn I feel like I can and will beat anyone.

Third, tennis requires a solid, well-rounded set of skills. Footwork, forehand and backhand strokes, correct technique for hitting shots in each area of the court, and total court coverage are just some of the skills the game requires. If a player's skills are underdeveloped, a good opponent will exploit the weakness.

This brings me to the fourth aspect of preparation to become a tennis champion—the tactical and strategic facets of the game. These facets include thinking the game, exploiting opponent's weakness, maximizing your strengths, playing the game smart—in short, winning tennis.

Tennis Tactics: Winning Patterns of Play is the first book to present all the possible patterns of play in singles tennis, broken down according to areas of the court. These patterns will help you better understand when and where to hit, look for, and anticipate shots from your opponent. The accompanying drills will help you execute and refine your strategic game plan. Hit more winners, become a champion, read and use *Tennis Tactics*.

Jim Courier

Preface

Accomplished players tend to develop strategically sound patterns of playing tennis that they like and feel confident executing. These patterns are simply a series of shots that is repeated over and over. The national coaching staff of the USTA has long theorized that practice sessions could be made more effective and fun if players were taught to practice their favorite patterns daily. But until now, there has never been a book showing players and coaches how to develop these patterns consciously and reinforce them with specific drills.

If you play tennis, keep score, and want to improve your play, then *Tennis Tactics: Winning Patterns of Play* will help you! Coaches, too, will find the patterns demonstrated in this book helpful in simplifying the game for players and in setting up practice sessions that have a clear purpose. Every player you coach will love learning the secrets of strategy used by the pros that make the game look so easy.

Part I of *Tennis Tactics* shows you how to choose the best patterns of play for your game. Once you've settled on the patterns that will work best for you, you can choose a style of play that is based on the strategies and tactical principles discussed in chapters 1 and 2. The next four parts of the book describe *backcourt*, *midcourt*, *net play*, and *defensive* patterns. These parts contain chapters that are paired. One chapter illustrates the patterns to use from that area of the court, and the companion chapter shows the drills to practice these patterns. In all, the easy-to-read illustrations introduce you to 58 patterns of play and 63 companion drills for practice. The cross-referenced Pattern Finder chart at the back of the book helps you locate the shot combinations you want to study and incorporate into your game.

Along with this book, you may want to order the video, *USTA's Winning Patterns of Play,* which is also available from Human Kinetics. The video shows tennis stars such as Pete Sampras, Andre Agassi,

Mary Joe Fernandez, Monica Seles, Chanda Rubin, Lindsay Davenport, and Michael Chang using their favorite patterns in actual match play at the U.S. Open and then features young players from the USTA Player Development Program performing drills based on professional patterns. To order the video, call 800-747-4457 (U.S.) or 217-351-5076 (outside the U.S.).

Tennis Tactics will help you play better tennis. You'll love this simple approach for play and practice. Whether you're an all-court specialist, a counterpuncher, an aggressive baseliner, or a serve-and-volleyer, your style of play will improve by using these patterns and drills. Soon you'll play like the pros!

Acknowledgments

Much of the collection, preparation, and editing of the material in this book was accomplished by the untiring efforts of USTA staff member Linda P. Jusiewicz. USTA Directors of Coaching Lynne Rolley and Nick Saviano coordinated the efforts of our sport science and coaching staffs in identifying key patterns of play and practical drills to go with them. The teamwork of the coaching staff in achieving consensus and closure on the project is much appreciated.

Members of the USTA staff who were involved in this project include:

Lynne Rolley
Stan Smith
Lew Brewer
Carol Watson
Jai DiLouie
Eric Amend

Nick Saviano
Tom Gullikson
Paul Roetert
Rodney Harmon
John Benson
Ken Herrmann

—Ronald B. Woods
Director of Player Development
United States Tennis Association

Key to Court Diagrams

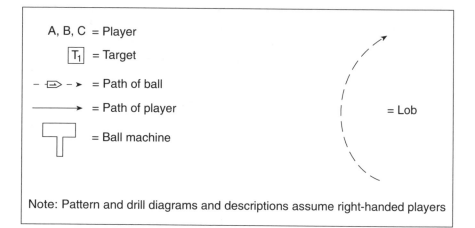

A, B, C = Player

$\boxed{T_1}$ = Target

– ⊏⊐→ ► = Path of ball

———► = Path of player

⊤ = Ball machine

= Lob

Note: Pattern and drill diagrams and descriptions assume right-handed players

PART I

Patterns of Singles Play

Chapters 1 and 2 review fundamentals of tennis strategy and show you how they apply to the patterns of play that are the basis for this book.

Fundamentals, again? You've been hearing about fundamentals from the day you hit your first forehand. So, no one blames you for being tempted to skip these chapters and get right to the heart of this book. But don't.

All winning tennis strategy—including the strategies behind the 58 patterns of play you'll learn in this book—are based on the principles of high-percentage tennis reviewed in chapter 1. To be sure, you know these strategies. If you play smart tennis, you apply them every day. But when is the last time you *consciously* thought about them?

Similarly, once you read through chapter 2 and the following chapters of this book, you may find that you have been unconsciously using some of the patterns we describe in your match play. But when was the last time you ever practiced a pattern of play? Never, we'll bet.

To become a brilliant tactician, you'll consciously want to plan your own patterns of play before each point in a match. You'll also constantly want to analyze your opponent's unconscious patterns of play. To accomplish this, ground yourself in the *fundamentals*.

 **Chapter 1**

Principles of Pattern Play

Tennis points are made of a sequence of shots. When you repeat a particular sequence of shots, your game begins to take on the form of a series of patterns of play. That's why the coaching staff of the USTA has devised a system of tennis drills based on the patterns tennis players use. Before you work through the patterns, however, it's imperative that you understand the basis for them. All of the patterns you'll find in this book are built on several strategic principles that have been well tested over time. Once you understand each of the principles reviewed in this chapter and experiment with them on the tennis court, you will begin to see the beauty of the patterns we recommend.

TENNIS IS A GAME OF ERRORS

At every level of play, 85 percent of points in tennis are lost as the result of an error. Naturally it follows that only a mere 15 percent are earned by winning shots. The secret then to winning tennis is to get your opponent in trouble and force her to take a risky shot.

Between highly skilled players, errors often occur because of accurate placement, power, or disguising of the shot. At every level of play, unforced errors are a significant part of every match, usually due to a poor choice of shots or faulty technique. If you can reduce your unforced errors just a bit and force a few from your opponent, the odds will be heavily in your favor.

KEYS TO REDUCING ERRORS

- Your first task on every shot is to clear the net. If you and your opponent are both at the baseline, aim your shot three to five feet above the net to eliminate errors into the net and insure good depth on your shots.

- Aim the ball well inside the lines to give yourself some margin for error. Even top professional players know the huge risk of trying to hit a line. Measure in six feet from the sideline and six feet from the baseline to mark a target for your groundstrokes that gives you a safety margin. See figure 1.1.

- Whenever you are in trouble during a point and forced to play a defensive shot, aim your shot high, deep, and crosscourt so that you can recover for the next shot.

- Early in the point, hit your shots deep crosscourt or deep down the middle. This reduces your chance of error and keeps your opponent on the defense.

- Movement to the ball and early preparation are the keys to consistent strokes. Aim to hit every ball in your strike zone (about waist high) and be well balanced at contact.

- It is generally safer to direct a ball back to the direction it came from rather than changing the angle. For example, the safest return of a crosscourt forehand is a return crosscourt. Only change the direction of a ball that you can control and are in good position to attack.

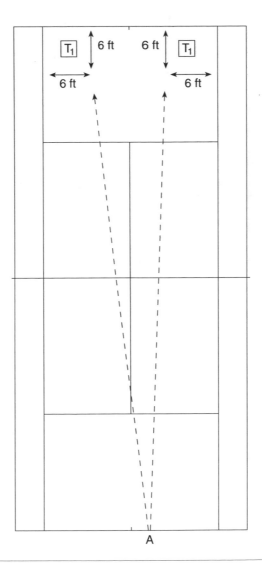

Figure 1.1 Six feet in from the sideline and six feet in front of the baseline are the aim points for the majority of groundstrokes.

HIT TO THE OPEN COURT

Once you have developed your tennis skills to the level where you can consistently direct most shots over the net and into the court, you are ready to aim the ball away from your opponent. Because your opponent cannot cover all possible angles at once, there will always be an opening. You may be able to hit the ball out of her reach for a winning shot. At the very least, you will force her to run to the ball and complicate her task of returning your shot. Your chances of hitting a winning shot increase markedly when you move into the midcourt or get to the net because your opponent will have less time to react and chase down your shot.

HIT BEHIND YOUR OPPONENT

During a point, your opponent will expect you to aim for the open court, particularly if you've managed to hit some forcing shots or even outright winners. As your opponent begins to anticipate your shot and perhaps lean a bit in that direction, you should direct your next shot behind him. He will find it extremely difficult to change direction, regain his balance, and adjust to the oncoming ball.

This strategy is particularly effective against players who are very quick at moving side to side, particularly if they anticipate your shot to the open court. It also works well when you have drawn your opponent very wide to one side and she is hustling back toward the center of the court to protect the wide-open court.

USE ANGLES TO OPEN THE COURT

Most players are taught to hit groundstrokes deep into the opponent's backcourt to keep him from attacking on a short ball. Although this is sound basic strategy, you also need to use the angles of the court side to side to open up areas into which you can direct winning shots or exploit your opponent's weaker side. By hitting some baseline drives sharply crosscourt, you will force him to play the return from outside the sideline and you can direct the next ball to a wide-open court.

If you play most of your tennis on relatively fast, hard surfaces, it is easy to fall into the trap of hitting most of your shots straight and deep. Watch the best clay court players to see how they use the angles by taking the ball early and aiming crosscourt to pull their opponent wide and off the court.

MOVE YOUR OPPONENT AROUND THE COURT

Mixing up your shots by varying the speed, depth, placement, and spin will challenge your opponent on every point. Just as a successful pitcher in baseball changes the speed, spin, and location of his pitches to confuse the batter, you should present your opponent with a wide variety of shots that are well disguised.

Many of your opponents will frustrate you with their steadiness during rallies unless you can force them to cover a lot of the court. Your opponent will need a great deal of athletic skill, good balance, and efficient movement to reach a series of well-placed strokes and respond with an offensive shot that is trouble for you. Even if your opponent is able to respond to your placements, chances are that over time, she will become fatigued and unable to reach a few balls.

At most levels of playing skill, the secret of moving your opponent around the court is to include up and back movement along with the more typical side-to-side moves. You might find it effective to begin the point with a deep baseline shot, followed by a short-angle or a drop shot that forces her to move forward at full speed. Your next shot can be a drive to the other side or perhaps a lob over her head. After a few all-out sprints up and back and side to side, your unlucky opponent will probably be thinking that she is in for a difficult match.

ADJUST TO YOUR OPPONENT

One of the great attractions of tennis is the challenge of probing for your opponent's weaknesses and then exploiting them. If you suspect he has a weak, defensive backhand, you should serve to the backhand and hit groundstrokes to the backhand until he presents you with an error or a weak shot that you can attack.

On the other hand, if you discover that your opponent has a favorite shot that he relies on to win points and force the play, you have to neutralize that shot. A hard flat serve such as Pete Sampras's can be negated simply by moving your position a few feet farther behind the baseline so that you have more time to prepare for the return. If your opponent has an effective kick serve with heavy spin that causes it to bounce high out of your hitting zone, move in a few feet to return it as it is rising with a firm drive or a chip shot at his feet.

ADJUST TO THE CONDITIONS

Sun, wind, temperature, and humidity all affect the play of tennis matches. Experience in coping with these conditions is invaluable, so you have to practice and play in all kinds of weather. You'll learn how to adjust your shots in the wind, hit more topspin with the wind at your back, and aim higher and deeper when hitting into the wind. Lobs and drop shots work well with the wind in your face. You'll find that lobbing to an opponent when the sun is in his eyes gives you a good chance of winning the point.

HOW PATTERNS CAN HELP

The next chapter introduces you to the patterns of play recommended by the USTA coaching staff and shows you how to select the patterns that will apply directly to your individual style of play. These patterns, based on the sound strategic principles we've just discussed, will help you get the most out of your shots. Match play will become automatic. Your shot selection during a point will make sense, and you'll literally put yourself in the best possible position to win the point.

 ***Chapter 2***

Patterns of Play

What kind of game do you play? Are you a serve-and-volleyer, an aggressive baseliner, a counterpuncher, or an all-court player? Over the years, USTA coaches have determined that each type of game depends on the mastery of different shot selection patterns. So, although there are a number of patterns upon which to base your game (and subsequently, a number of drills to reinforce these patterns), only certain patterns will benefit you most directly. Therefore, the perfect patterns for you depend on the game you play. That's why this chapter first discusses styles of play. After you determine your style, use the remaining advice in the chapter and the Pattern Finder on pages 231-234 to see which patterns will make your game as effective as it can be.

You will find it helpful to identify and practice particular shot sequences that emphasize your strengths as a player and minimize your weaknesses. As you achieve mastery of certain patterns over time, you will gain confidence as a player and find it easier to develop a successful game plan for each match. Your tennis game will begin to take on your personal style of play, and it will be based on sound principles of strategy and tactics.

At every level of playing skill, you should understand the strategy of the game you want to play and then work on the skills that will let you apply your plan. Strategy in tennis is based on

- the principles of percentage play (as discussed in chapter 1),
- your strengths and weaknesses, and
- your opponent's strengths and weaknesses.

PLAYER STRENGTHS AND WEAKNESSES

In addition to playing high-percentage tennis, you need to plan your strategy around your own and your opponent's strengths and weaknesses. Tennis can become much like a chess match, with each of you mounting a series of attacks and defenses.

In practice, you need to inventory your tennis skills and identify them as strengths or weaknesses. Next you need to adopt one of the four basic styles of play with some individual variation. The four basic styles of play are

- counterpuncher,
- aggressive baseliner,
- all-court player, and
- serve-and-volleyer.

Counterpunchers

A counterpuncher's game is defined by excellent movement skills and quickness as well as steady groundstrokes, accurate passing shots, and well-controlled lobs. Your job as a counterpuncher is to retrieve every ball, which means excellent conditioning is an absolute must. Counterpunchers have that "never say die" attitude where consistency is the name of the game. Role models include Michael Chang, Sergio Bruguera, Arantxa Sanchez-Vicario, and Amanda Coetzer.

Aggressive Baseliners

If you are an aggressive baseliner, your physical characteristics are defined by quickness, muscular strength, and endurance; your competitive personality is often that of a risk taker. In addition to building at least one shot into a weapon that you can count on in any situation, you will need to develop penetrating baseline groundstrokes that land deep in the court. Precise footwork and steady balance are also essential characteristics of this style of play. Role models include Steffi Graf, Monica Seles, Lindsay Davenport, Jim Courier, Andre Agassi, and Andrei Medvedev.

All-Court Players

All-court players are typically athletic, quick, and have excellent movement skills that are enhanced by endurance and high-level fitness. All-courters are shotmakers who can shift easily from defense to offense, probing until their opponent's weakness is exposed. If you don't have a single outstanding weapon, but play well from every part of the court and love to make something happen, you most likely will have success as an all-courter. Typical role models include Pete Sampras, Michael Stich, Jana Novotna, and Gabriela Sabatini.

Serve-and-Volleyers

If you're on the tall side, possess good reach and agility, a powerful overhead, a soft touch, and are most comfortable at the net, you have the makings of a serve-and-volleyer. A big serve and a punishing overhead smash are crucial to this style of game. Serve-and-volley players usually have an aggressive on-court personality and play a high-risk game. Role models include Martina Navratilova, Lori McNeil, Stefan Edberg, and Boris Becker.

The Patterns to Fit Your Style

The Pattern Finder on pages 231-234 lists the 58 patterns described in this book. You will find that the list is subdivided according to your position on the court. That is, you'll find backcourt patterns, midcourt patterns, net play patterns, and defensive play patterns. Backcourt patterns are further subdivided into serve and return patterns, return of serve patterns, and groundstroke patterns.

That's a lot of patterns. However, within each style of play described are certain shot patterns that are the "bread and butter" of that style. Once you've chosen or identified your style, refer to figure 2.1 to see which patterns are best for you to perfect.

Don't be overwhelmed by the fact that each style of play is represented by quite a number of patterns. Even at the highest levels of the game, players typically use only a few patterns that match their physical characteristics, stroke technique, and personality. They

PATTERNS AND STYLES

Every style of play can be defined by the type of shot patterns it typically uses. For example, serve-and-volley players will focus on more net play patterns than will baseliners. Let the table below point you toward the patterns that are right for your game.

Key Patterns and Drills for Each Style of Play

STYLE OF PLAY	KEY PATTERNS
Counterpuncher	
Return of serve	6-13, 17-18
Groundstrokes	19-26
Defensive play	43-58
Aggressive baseliner	
Serve	1-5
Return of serve	6-18
Groundstrokes	19-26
Midcourt play	27-28, 31-33
Defensive play	43-58
All-court player[1]	
Midcourt play	27-34
Net play	35-37
Serve-and-volleyer	
Serve	1-5
Return of serve	14-16
Midcourt play	27-34
Net play	35-42

[1]By definition, all-court players must master all 58 patterns and may use all the drills in this book that support them; however, all-courters should especially emphasize the aggressive midcourt and net play patterns to close out points.

Figure 2.1   The perfect patterns for your style of play.

emphasize those shot sequences in every practice and aim for flaw-less execution.

APPLYING PATTERNS TO TENNIS TODAY

You'll enjoy watching the top players more if you notice their typical patterns, how the opponent tries to neutralize them, and the adjustments each player makes during the match.

In professional tennis, players are often evenly matched in skills. If you wander over to observe players on the practice courts of a professional tournament, you will have difficulty picking out the top players just by watching them trade forehands and backhands. What separates players at every level is their ability to hit sequences of shots and the preciseness and consistency of these patterns.

Your practices should be considerably more efficient if you use the type of drills that are presented in this book. After all, each time you practice a sequence that is part of your game plan, you are adding an element of automatic shotmaking that will be there when you're feeling pressure in a match. The shot pattern should become an automatic response to the situation you're presented with during the point.

HOW TO PRACTICE PATTERNS

Once you identify the patterns you need to practice, you'll find chapters 4, 6, 8, 10, and 12 an invaluable source of drills designed to help you perfect your patterns. But you must then translate your plan into effective on-court sessions. The following suggestions will help you plan efficient practice sessions based on the accepted principles of learning motor skills. The amount of time you spend practicing your tennis skills is up to you, but keep in mind that "practice does not make perfect"—perfect practice does.

HIGH VS. LOW VARIABILITY

Because playing the game of tennis requires you to adjust on every exchange to a wide variety of shots, the drills you do in practice should mirror those challenges. Your opponent will confront you with shots that make you run, stretch, lean, or move out of the way. The pace, spin, and depth of the oncoming ball will further complicate your response. The most efficient learning requires that you understand the importance of practicing shots with wide variability so that you feel confident during match play in handling your opponent's tricks.

Many players practice a certain shot over and over again from a ball that is fed to them at the same pace and location. For example, hitting repetitive volleys at shoulder height from a coach's feed will not help you learn to deal with difficult passing shots that you may face in a match. To gain confidence in your technique, after the initial learning period, have a partner or coach feed you shots that force you to bend low, stretch wide, and adjust to a variety of shot speeds.

Dead-Ball vs. Live-Ball Feeds

In practice, many coaches repeatedly feed balls out of their hand to players to produce a consistent and predictable sequence of shots. The limitation of this type of practice is that you never get to deal with a series of live balls that are in play. This limits your ability to anticipate shots and make the adjustments to the ball that you need to make during match play.

Drills vs. Playing the Game

The drills in this book can help you learn to play better at a faster rate than just relying on playing sets. But don't make the mistake of thinking that drills can substitute completely for match play. In fact, at higher levels of play, you should probably aim for drilling 25 percent of the time, modified play 25 percent, and normal match play about 50 percent.

If you are a beginning player, the percentage of time spent drilling might be increased a bit until you become more confident in your skills and your responses to certain situations become more automatic. However, don't drill so much that you lose the fun and excitement of playing the game.

Practice Sequences

The most efficient sequence in learning a new pattern of play is as follows:

1. Learn and practice each shot in the sequence by itself until you can consistently perform the skill. During this time, you should emphasize the proper technique and execution of the shot.
2. The second step is to perform each shot repetitively until the movement becomes an automatic physical response. This is called "grooving" a shot and is best done from a predictably fed ball. You should be thinking of only one or two technique tips that you've found are the keys to successful execution of the shot.
3. The third step is to try the sequence of shots in the pattern just as they are likely to occur during a point. Again, you'll have the most success early on if you start with fed balls that are predictable.
4. As soon as possible, you should proceed to a live-ball situation where the ball is in play. The *majority* of your practice time should be spent on this type of drill so that you become accustomed to a live-ball sequence that you'll face in match play.
5. If you become frustrated at your inability to complete the pattern, you may need to return to a dead-ball sequence that is a bit easier, or perhaps you'll need some technical help from a coach on the execution of a particular shot.
6. Finally, you should set up some gamelike situations with particular limitations that will help you work on certain patterns of play. For example, you might play a set during which you are required to serve and volley on every first serve or only on first serves to the ad court. Another popular modified game is to allow only one serve and require the receiver to attack the serve and come to net or go for a winning drive. See pages 16-17 for tips on how to create modified game situations that will spice up your practice sessions.
7. After you've progressed through the sequence of learning and drilling, be sure you play normal competitive sets and work on certain patterns during play. Applying the patterns you've learned to the game situation is the final test to measure your skill.

MODIFIED GAME SITUATIONS

In addition to practicing the drills that are suggested on the following pages, an excellent practice technique is to play points or game situations with a slight variation in the rules of play. The modification of the rules will force you to work on a particular aspect of your game while still allowing you the fun of playing and competing.

One-Serve Tennis

Play a normal set of tennis, but the server is allowed only one serve. This will quickly expose any weakness on the second serve. The receiver should look for every opportunity to take advantage of weak, shallow serves and attack.

Three-Serve Tennis

Play a normal set of tennis, but the server is allowed up to three serves on every point. Since the first serve is virtually a free one, the server should try for an ace or winner on every first serve. If he misses the first, he still has the normal two serves coming on each point. This is a great game for those who are too timid on the first serve.

Ace Wins Game

Another good way to reward risk taking on the first serve is to award the game to the server anytime she is able to server an ace—that is, one that her opponent cannot touch. It also keeps the receiver on her toes defending because she does not want to lose an entire game by giving up just one ace.

Double Fault or Return Error Loses Game

Play a normal set with conventional scoring except that at any time during the set, a player who commits a double fault or misses a return of serve loses the game, regardless of the score. This is a particularly good game to stress consistency of play on the first two shots of any point.

All Returns Crosscourt

Play a normal set except the receiver must hit all returns crosscourt. Use the center service line and its imaginary extension along with the singles sideline as boundaries to determine a good crosscourt return. This will help you get in the habit of hitting high-percentage returns.

Ten-Point Games—One Server

Play points alternately to the deuce and ad service boxes until one player earns 10 points and wins by at least 2 points. Then switch the roles of server and receiver for the next 10 point game. As a variation, the server begins every point by serving into the deuce court. This will be a real test of your serving ability and may expose a weakness serving to one side of the court.

One Set—Same Server

Play an entire set with one player serving every game of the set. This will give both players a chance to concentrate on and experiment with one critical skill—either serving or returning. During the set, it is important for both players to vary their shots to keep their opponent from anticipating the play.

Handicap—One Serve

Players of slightly different skill levels can create exciting competition by restricting the better player to one serve and allowing the other player to have the normal two serves.

THE NEXT STEP

This chapter has helped you understand which patterns might enhance your personal style of play. As you begin to review the following chapters, highlight the specific patterns that you want to concentrate on to improve your game. As you study the patterns you select, be sure to analyze the suggested sequence of shots and see if they make sense to you strategically. The strategic principle of each pattern should be evident: You are trying to capitalize on your strengths, exploit your opponent's weakness, move your opponent, open up the court, hit behind your opponent, or some combination that will give you the best chance of winning the point.

It probably makes sense to begin with backcourt patterns that include serve, return of serve, and groundstrokes. After all, points always begin with those shots, and in fact most points end after just a few shots, especially on faster court surfaces.

Along with the description and illustration of each pattern, you'll find a brief explanation of the *objective* of that pattern and a list of the drills to practice it. Use the drills to "groove" your shots into the pattern so that you'll own that pattern in match play.

 *PART II*

Backcourt Patterns and Drills

Part II emphasizes patterns and drills designed to show you how to practice shots from the backcourt in a way that will prepare you for playing matches. These patterns and accompanying drills will focus on making your serves and returns sharper and your groundstrokes more effective. Take the time to understand the theory behind each pattern so that your practice makes sense to you. Generally, you'll see that backcourt patterns are based on the strategic principle that crosscourt shots from the baseline give you the least risk for error.

 *Chapter 3*

Serve and Return Patterns

The serve and return of serve may be the most important shots in tennis because every point begins with them. Your serve should be a weapon that earns points outright or at least forces a weak return. Patterns 1 through 5 in this chapter describe service and first shot combinations that help you dictate the point. Equally important is your ability to return your opponent's serve to neutralize her weapon. Patterns 6 through 18 provide you with "mental maps" that remind you to hit your returns deep and be alert for weak second serves that you can attack. Chapter 4 will provide you with 13 drills that will reinforce the patterns displayed in this chapter.

PATTERN **1**

Deuce Court
Serve Wide to Open the Court

Objective: Hit the second shot (groundstroke) to the open court for a winner or an approach shot.

Drills: 4.1, 4.2, 4.3, 4.4, 4.9

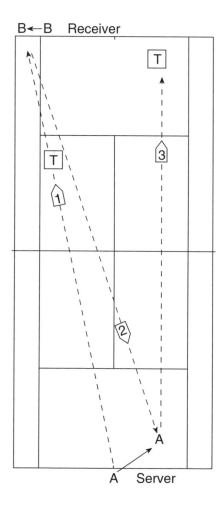

PATTERN 2

Ad Court

Serve Wide to Open the Court

Objective: Hit the second shot (groundstroke) to the open court for a winner or an approach shot.

Drills: 4.1, 4.2, 4.3, 4.4, 4.9

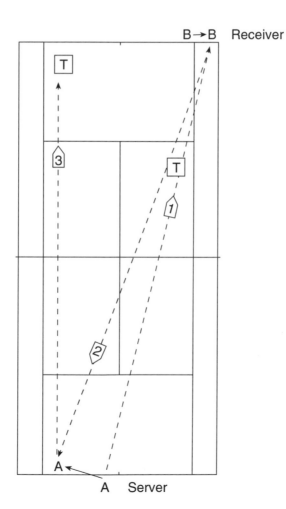

B→B   Receiver

A   Server

PATTERN 3

Deuce Court

Serve to the "T" to Reduce the Angles

Objective: Hit the second shot (groundstroke) down the line or to your opponent's weaker side.

Drills: 4.1, 4.2, 4.3, 4.4, 4.5, 4.9, 4.10

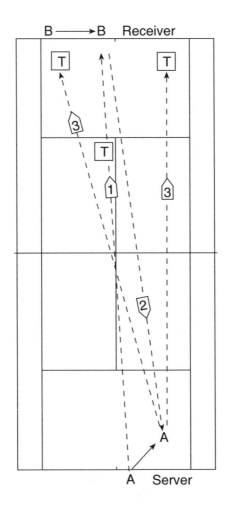

PATTERN 4

Ad Court

Serve to the "T" to Reduce the Angles

Objective: Hit the second shot (groundstroke) down the line or to your opponent's weaker side.

Drills: 4.1, 4.2, 4.3, 4.4, 4.5, 4.9, 4.10

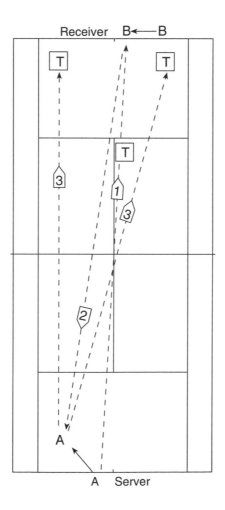

PATTERN 5

Both Courts
Serve at the Body to Jam the Receiver

Objective: Expect a short, weak return. Hit a forcing second shot (groundstroke) or an outright winner.

Drills: 4.2, 4.5, 4.9, 4.10, 4.11

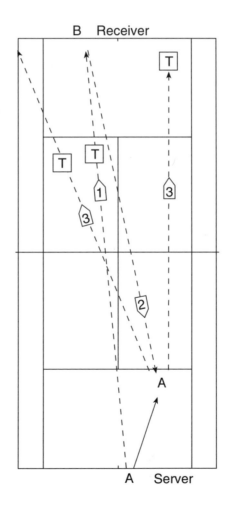

PATTERN **6**

Deuce Court—Against a Wide Serve
Return Deep Crosscourt

Objective: Aim for depth and safety to begin a crosscourt rally.

Drills: 4.6, 4.8, 4.9, 4.11

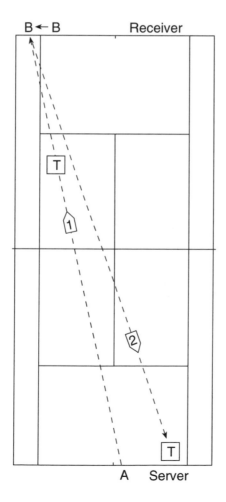

PATTERN **7**

Ad Court—Against a Wide Serve
Return Deep Crosscourt

Objective: Aim for depth and safety to begin a crosscourt rally.

Drills: 4.6, 4.8, 4.9, 4.11

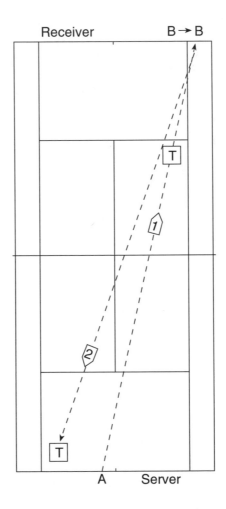

PATTERN **8**

Deuce Court—Against an Extreme Wide Serve

Return Deep Down the Line

Objective: Aim for depth and force the server to move quickly to cover the down-the-line shot. You may want to force your opponent to hit her weak shot.

Drills: 4.6, 4.7, 4.8, 4.9, 4.11

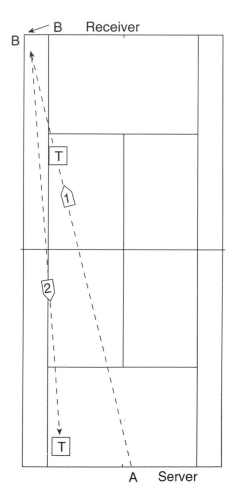

PATTERN **9**

Ad Court—Against an Extreme Wide Serve
Return Deep Down the Line

Objective: Aim for depth and force the server to move quickly to cover the down-the-line shot. You may want to force your opponent to hit his weak shot.

Drills: 4.6, 4.7, 4.8, 4.9, 4.11

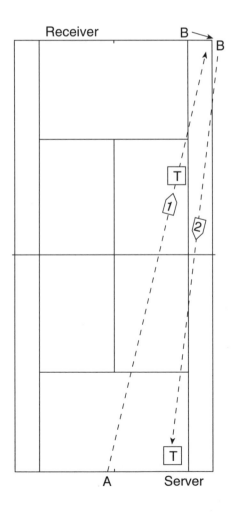

PATTERN **10**

Deuce Court—Against a Serve to the "T"

Return Deep Down the Middle

Objective: Aim for depth and safety by hitting to the largest area of the court. Increase consistency by aiming high over the net.

Drills: 4.6, 4.8, 4.9, 4.11

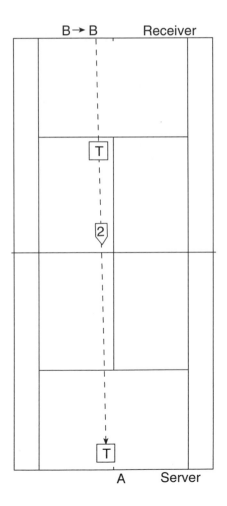

PATTERN **11**

Ad Court—Against a Serve to the "T"
Return Deep Down the Middle

Objective: Aim for depth and safety by hitting to the largest area of the court. Increase consistency by aiming high over the net.

Drills: 4.6, 4.8, 4.9, 4.11

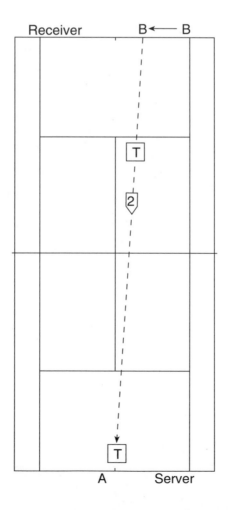

PATTERN **12**

Deuce Court—Against a Serve to the "T"

Return Deep Down the Line

Objective: Aim deep to put the server in a defensive position.

Drills: 4.6, 4.8, 4.9, 4.11

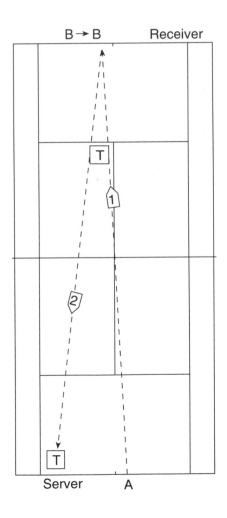

PATTERN **13**

Ad Court—Against a Serve to the "T"

Return Deep Down the Line

Objective: Aim deep to put the server in a defensive position.

Drills: 4.6, 4.8, 4.9, 4.11

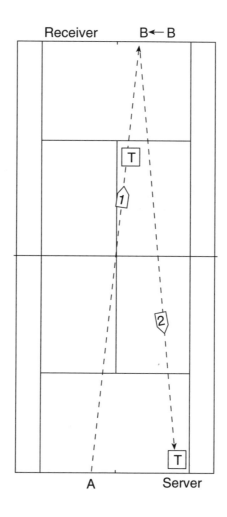

PATTERN **14**

Against a Short, Weak Serve

Hit a Forcing Shot Down the Line

Objective: Hit an aggressive drive to attack a weakness and elicit a weak reply.

Drills: 4.10, 4.11, 4.12

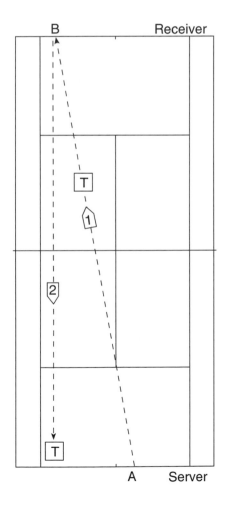

PATTERN **15**

Against a Short, Weak Serve

Hit a Forcing Shot Crosscourt

Objective: Hit an aggressive drive to attack a weakness and elicit a weak reply.

Drills: 4.10, 4.11

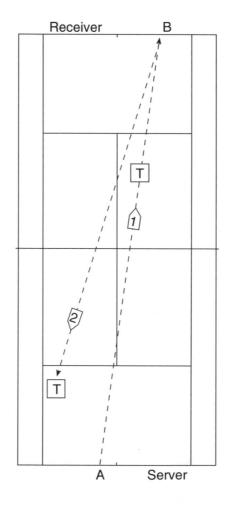

PATTERN **16**

Against a Short, Weak Serve

Chip or Drive Down the Line and Come to the Net

Objective: Hit an approach shot down the line and follow the ball to the net. Volley the next shot to the open court.

Drill: 4.12

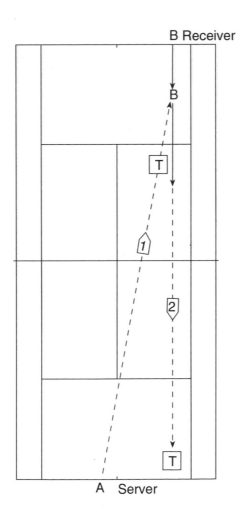

PATTERN **17**

Against a Serve-and-Volleyer

Return Low at the Server's Feet

Objective: To force the server to make a difficult first volley from a ball that is below the level of the net. Go for a passing shot on the next ball.

Drill: 4.13

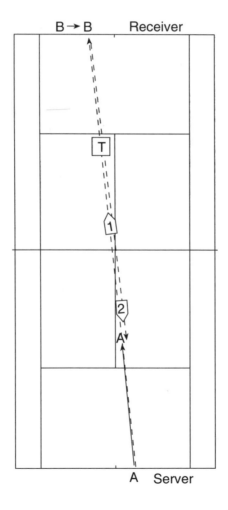

PATTERN **18**

Against a Serve-and-Volleyer
Return Down the Line

Objective: If the server closes fast, does not split-step, or does not follow the ball after a wide serve, the down-the-line shot will catch her when she's unable to change direction to play the volley.

Drill: 4.13

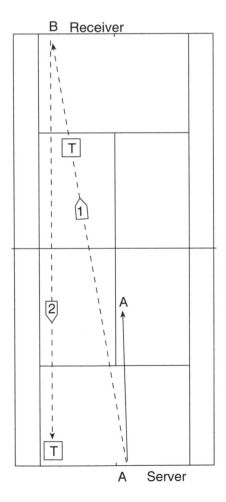

 **Chapter 4**

Serve and Return Drills

The serve and return drills offer a variety of ways you can practice patterns with a partner or even with several players on one court. Try these drills in sequence, since they are ordered to some degree by difficulty of execution. Once you feel confident with most of these drills, choose your favorite patterns for serving and receiving and play some practice sets using only those patterns.

DRILL **4.1**

 Around the World

Patterns

1 - 4

Category: *Serve*

Purpose: To develop consistency and placement in serving.

Equipment: Ball hopper with tennis balls; rope or chalk to divide the court.

Level: Beginner and up.

Time: 10 to 15 minutes. This is a good warm-up activity.

Procedure: Player A hits two serves from position A_1 to the outside and then the inside of the service box. If successful, she moves back to position A_2, then A_3. She then moves to A_4, A_5, and A_6. Her objective is to execute all 12 serves successfully. Any missed serve requires that she start over from position A_1.

Coaching Points:

- Emphasize technique and placement.
- This drill will add some pressure and challenge.

DRILL **4.1**

Around the World

Patterns

1 - 4

A_4 A_1

A_5 A_2

A_6 A_3

DRILL **4.2**

 Target Serving

Patterns

1 - 5

Category: *Serve*

Purpose: To develop placement of the serve.

Equipment: Targets—may be cones, towels, hoops, or racquet bags; ball hopper with tennis balls.

Level: Advanced beginner to professional.

Time: 15 minutes or until there is a winner.

Procedure: Players A and B serve a first and second serve to targets T_1, T_2, T_3, and T_4 in succession for a total of eight serves. Players score 1 point for each serve that hits the target. Players then retrieve the balls and return to the end of the line facing the opposite service box. The first player to earn 10 points is the winner. Deduct 1 point any time a serve goes into the net.

Coaching Points:

- Emphasize a deliberate ritual in preparing to serve.
- Stress consistency of the ball toss and disguise of direction

DRILL **4.2**

Target Serving

Patterns

1 - 5

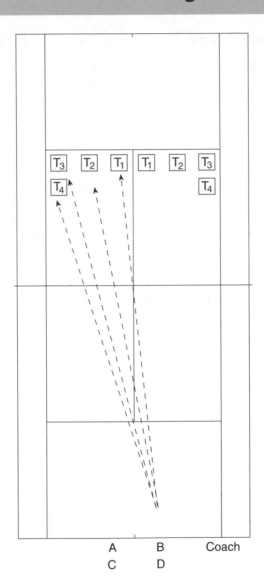

DRILL **4.3**

 Pressure Serving

Patterns

1 - 4

Category: *Serve*

Purpose: To test serving skill in a pressure situation.

Equipment: An audience of teammates or others to create pressure. Encourage the audience to cheer for players as they would in a match.

Level: Beginner to advanced.

Time: 5 minutes per player for one trial.

Procedure: Create the following scenario: "It's the third set of a crucial match and player A leads 6 games to 5. If she can hit four first serves in, the odds are she'll win the match." Have each player in turn attempt the four serves in succession. If all four serves land in, you've got a winner. If a player misses on the first serve, she must go to another court and hit 40 practice serves before trying again. For a miss on the second serve, the penalty is 30 serves, and so on.

Beginner: Serves may land anywhere in the correct half of the service box.

Intermediate: Serves must land beyond the depth line (see drill diagram) in the correct half.

Advanced: To prevent soft serves, the ball must land beyond the power line (see drill diagram) on the second bounce.

Coaching Point:

- Remind players to take their time and perform their normal ritual before serving so as to relax and focus all their attention on the task.

DRILL **4.3**

Pressure Serving

Patterns

1 - 4

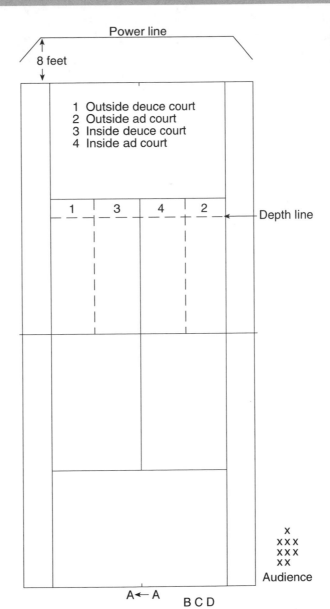

Power line

8 feet

1 Outside deuce court
2 Outside ad court
3 Inside deuce court
4 Inside ad court

| 1 | 3 | 4 | 2 |

Depth line

x
x x x
x x x
x x
Audience

A ← A   B C D

DRILL **4.4**

Opening the Court

Patterns

1 - 4

Category: *Serve*

Purpose: To practice wide serves to open up the court for the next shot.

Equipment: Target—may be cones, towels, hoops, or racquet bags.

Level: Intermediate to professional.

Time: 5 minutes to each service box.

Procedure: Server A hits a wide serve or an extremely wide serve. Receiver B returns crosscourt. The server hits the next shot aggressively to the open court. Player B tries to play the fourth shot back deep, and if he is successful, he earns a point. If he fails, the server scores a point.

Variations:

1. Switch sides to the ad court.
2. Switch the roles of server and receiver.

Coaching Points:

- To prevent the receiver from cheating toward the outside, the server should hit an occasional serve down the middle.
- Use a slice serve to pull the receiver wide out of the court.
- Step inside the baseline and play the ball early to hit a forcing shot crosscourt.
- Vary the size of targets to suit the level of play and ensure some success.

DRILL **4.4**

Opening the Court

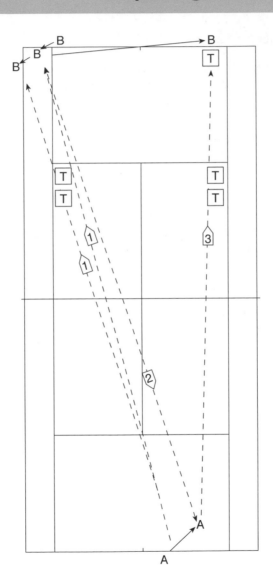

Patterns

1 - 4

DRILL **4.5**

 Serve and Hit Behind Opponent

Patterns

3 - 5

Category: *Serve*

Purpose: To pull the receiver to the middle of the court and then hit your second shot behind her.

Equipment: Targets.

Level: Intermediate to professional.

Time: After 10 successful serves and returns, players switch sides of the court.

Procedure: Player A serves to the inside of the service box to pull the receiver to the middle of the court. On the second shot, player A hits a deep forcing shot behind player B. As soon as the point is over, players C and D execute the same pattern to the ad court.

Coaching Points:

- To prevent the receiver from cheating toward the center, the server should hit an occasional serve wide.
- Emphasize moving into the court on the second shot to play the ball early and hit behind the receiver.

DRILL **4.5**

Serve and Hit Behind Opponent

Patterns

3 - 5

DRILL **4.6**

 Return—Deep Game

Patterns

6 - 13

Category: *Return of Serve*

Purpose: To practice deep returns into the court, emphasizing good net clearance to reduce errors and ensure good depth.

Equipment: A rope strung across the court approximately three to four feet above the height of the net.

Level: Beginner to professional.

Time: Until one set is completed.

Procedure: Players A and B are the serving team, players C and D the returning team. On the first point, player A serves to player C (two serves allowed), who must return the ball deep to the shaded area in the backcourt. If player C is successful, his team wins the point and the score is love-15. On the second point, player B serves to player D, and if the return fails, the score becomes 15-all. Continue the game to its conclusion. Players C and D become the serving team for the next game. Continue play until one set is complete.

Coaching Points:

- Emphasize variety and placement for the serving team.
- Emphasize consistency and good net clearance by the receiving team.

DRILL **4.6**

Return—Deep Game

Patterns

6 - 13

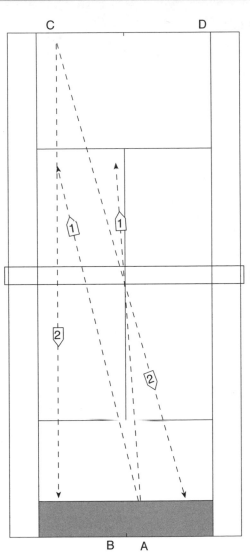

Rope 3 to 4 feet above net

DRILL **4.7**

 Cutting Off the Angle of Return

Patterns

8 and 9

Category: *Return of Serve*

Purpose: To practice moving forward on a diagonal path to cut off the extreme wide-angle serve and return it deep down the line.

Equipment: None

Level: Intermediate to professional.

Time: 10 minutes to each service box.

Procedure: *Two-shot drill.* Player A hits an extremely wide serve. Player B moves forward in a diagonal direction to intercept and returns the ball deep down the line.

Three-shot drill. Player A then hits a sharply angled crosscourt shot to the open court. After one trial, players A and B rotate out and players C and D replace them to attempt the identical pattern.

Variation: After about 10 minutes, players execute the same pattern to the ad court.

Coaching Points:

- Servers should emphasize moving forward to cut off serves.
- Receivers should use a topspin shot for safety on the crosscourt shot.

DRILL **4.7**

Cutting Off the Angle of Return

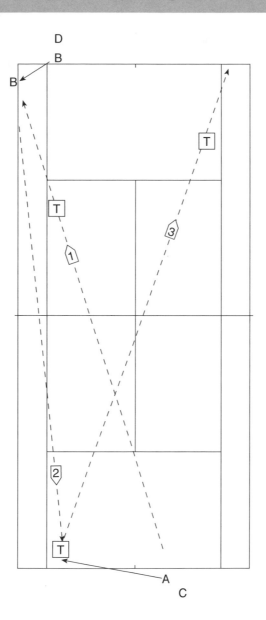

DRILL **4.8**

 Facing the Cannon

Patterns

6 - 13

Category: *Return of Serve*

Purpose: To handle high-speed serves and place the returns deep.

Equipment: None.

Level: Intermediate to professional.

Time: Each player should make 10 successful returns.

Procedure: The coach stands three feet inside the baseline to serve and delivers hard serves that vary in placement and spin. Player A returns three serves, first to target T_1, then T_2, then his choice. Player B then steps in for his turn. To add an element of competition, keep track of the number of successful returns for each player.

Variation: Repeat the drill to the ad court.

Coaching Points:

- Players should emphasize a quick shoulder turn and a short backswing.
- The coach may want to start the serve with the racquet behind the head to speed the drill.

DRILL **4.8**

Facing the Cannon

Patterns

6 - 13

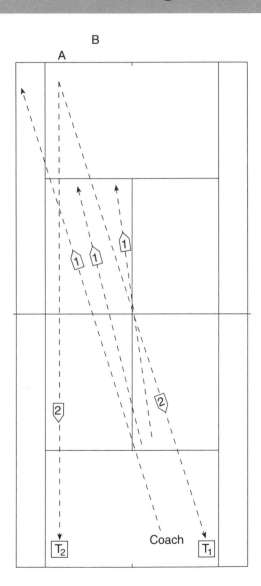

DRILL **4.9**

 Team Serving and Return

Patterns

1 - 13

Category: *Serve and Return*

Purpose: To develop consistency and placement on serves and consistency and depth on returns.

Equipment: None.

Level: Intermediate to advanced.

Time: 15 to 30 minutes.

Procedure: Player A tries two serves to any location in the deuce court. Player D tries to return each serve deep into the shaded area. The server loses 1 point if the serve is a fault. If the serve is good and the deep return is successful, 2 points are awarded to the receiving team. If the serve is good but the return fails to land deep, 2 points are awarded to the serving team. Player B follows in turn, serving to player E, and then player C serves to player F. The team score is cumulative until one team scores 21 points.

Variation:

1. Use the ad court.
2. Switch the serving and receiving teams.

Coaching Points:

- Emphasize technique on serves and returns.
- Encourage team spirit and reward the winning team.

DRILL **4.9**

Team Serving and Return

Patterns
1 - 13

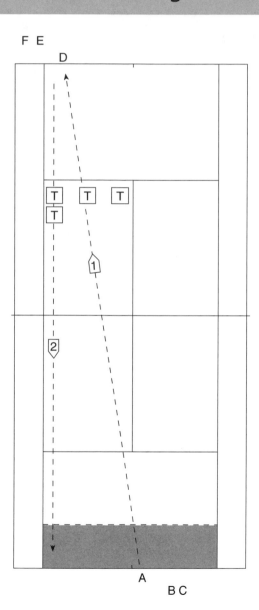

DRILL **4.10**

 Pound a Weakness

Patterns

3, 14, 15

Category: *Serve*

Purpose: To exploit an opponent's weakness on the backhand side; serve and then drive a succession of shots to the weakness.

Equipment: None.

Level: Intermediate to advanced.

Time: 15 minutes.

Procedure: Player A serves to player B's weak backhand or at the body to "jam" him. After a weak return, player A drives his second shot deep to player B's backhand and repeats that shot until he gets an error or can hit a winner to the open court.

Variation: If the opponent's weaker side is the forehand or if he is left-handed, adjust the pattern accordingly. Repeat the pattern beginning with the serve to the ad court.

Coaching Point:

- The server should use a slice serve into the body or a topspin kick serve to his opponent's obvious weakness on the backhand side.

DRILL **4.10**

Pound a Weakness

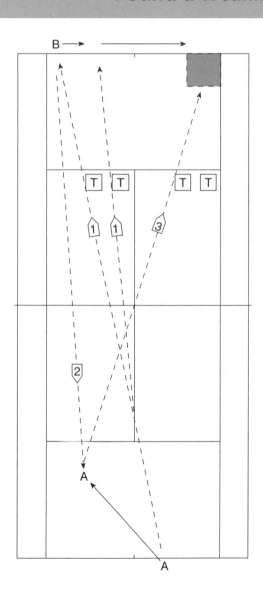

Patterns

3, 14, 15

DRILL **4.11**

 Punish the Server

Patterns

4 - 15

Category: *Return*

Purpose: To develop a punishing return of serve.

Equipment: A full ball hopper.

Level: Advanced to professional.

Time: 15 to 30 minutes.

Procedure: Coach serves a weak and shallow second serve. Player A moves forward to hit his strongest shot (usually a forehand) and hits an aggressive return to either target T_1 or target T_2. After one trial, player B takes a turn and is followed by players C and D in turn.

Variations:

1. Repeat the pattern in the deuce court.
2. Award points to individuals or team for successful aggressive returns.

Coaching Points:

- The receiver should move forward inside the baseline before the serve bounces.
- Emphasize playing the ball early off the bounce.

DRILL **4.11**

Punish the Server

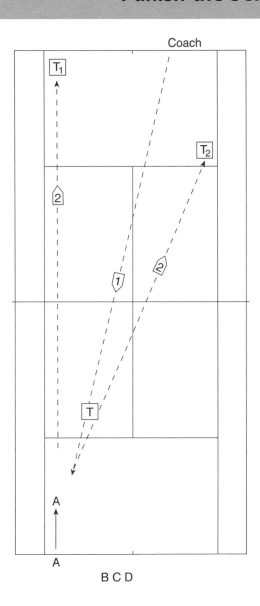

DRILL **4.12**

 ## Return—Attack Net

Patterns

14 and 16

Category: *Return*

Purpose: To attack a weak serve by coming to the net and hitting a winning volley.

Equipment: None.

Level: Intermediate to professional.

Time: The receiver should complete the pattern successfully 10 times to the ad court and 10 times to the deuce court.

Procedure: Player A moves inside the baseline and drives or chips the return of serve down the line, following the flight path of the ball and closing in to the net to finish the point with a volley to target T_1 or T_2. Player B should hit a moderately paced passing shot toward the middle of the court to allow player A to execute the winning volley.

Variation: Repeat the pattern to the ad court by hitting the return down the line on the other side of the court.

Coaching Points:

- Player A should start from a position inside the baseline by anticipating a weak serve. As player A closes toward the net, he must be sure to split-step and establish a position that bisects the angle of possible returns.
- Player B is only allowed to hit a passing shot (no lobs) to allow player A to play the winning volley.

Return—Attack Net

Patterns

14 and 16

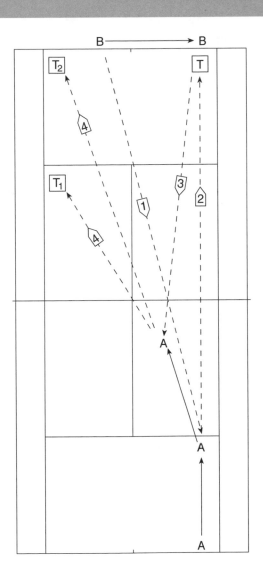

DRILL **4.13**

 Return Against a Net-Rusher

Patterns

17 and 18

Category: *Return*

Purpose: To hit low returns at the feet of the oncoming net-rusher.

Equipment: A rope strung across the court approximately three to four feet above the height of the net.

Level: Intermediate to professional.

Time: After 5 minutes, rotate player A to the receiving position. After 15 minutes, repeat the pattern in the ad court.

Procedure: Player A serves a second serve with spin and rushes the net. Player B returns the ball low below the rope at player A's feet. Player A hits a low volley or half-volley down the line, aiming for the deep target. After one trial, player C replaces player A in the serving role. To emphasize consistency and speed up the drill, the servers are allowed only one serve.

Coaching Points:

- The receiver should hit low returns with topspin or underspin to force the net-rusher to volley up.
- If the net-rusher closes fast, does not split-step, or does not follow the path of the ball on a wide serve, the receiver should hit the return down the line.

DRILL **4.13**

Return Against a Net-Rusher

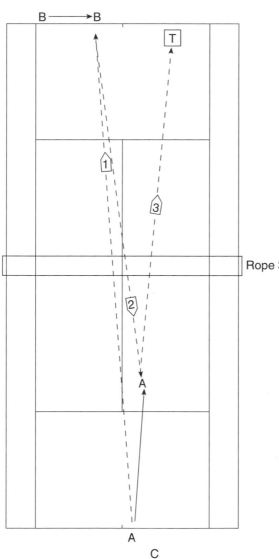

Rope 3 to 4 feet above net

 *Chapter 5*

Groundstroke Patterns

Every point in tennis begins with both players in the backcourt. After the serve and return, most points continue with an exchange of groundstrokes. Your task from the backcourt is to spar with your opponent by consistently returning the ball over the net and within the boundaries of the court. You should aim for steadiness and depth by adjusting the height of your shots and varying the amount of spin you apply to the ball. The hope is that your opponent will make an error before you do or will hit such a weak shot that you can attack.

The laws of physics dictate that to clear the net, the flight of the ball from your racquet must be upward. Patterns 19 through 25 mirror the principle of sound percentage tennis that suggests that most of your shots from the backcourt should be directed crosscourt toward the larger area of the court to reduce your chance of error until you get a short ball that you can attack. Pattern 26 deviates slightly from this strategy by suggesting that high, deep shots down the middle of the court may be answered with high, deep shots up the middle. Chapter 6 provides you with 12 drills that will groove the patterns you find in this chapter.

PATTERN **19**

Rally Crosscourt
Attack a Short Ball Down the Line

Objective: Keep the ball deep until you get a short ball, then attack the ball above the net by driving it down the line.

Drills: 6.1, 6.2, 6.3, 6.4, 6.5, 6.6

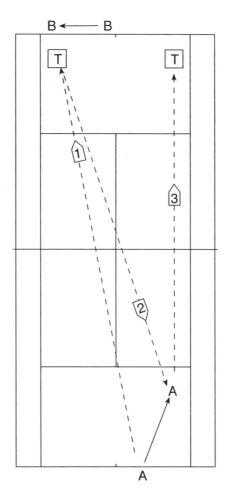

PATTERN **20**

Rally Crosscourt
Attack a Short Ball Crosscourt

Objective: If the ball lands in the outside third of the court and opens up an angle, drive the ball crosscourt and off the court.

Drills: 6.1, 6.3, 6.5, 6.6

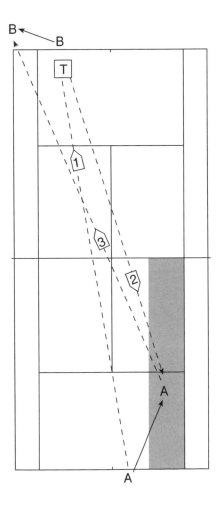

PATTERN **21**

Rally Crosscourt to Get Short, Wide Ball

Hit a Severe Angle

Objective: From a short, wide ball, hit a severely angled crosscourt shot with heavy topspin that draws your opponent off the court and direct the next ball to the open court.

Drills: 6.1, 6.3, 6.5, 6.7

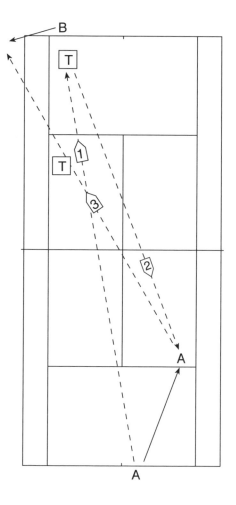

PATTERN **22**

From a Ball Down the Middle
Drive Inside-Out Through the Court

Objective: Step around a ball down the middle and drive an inside-out forehand through the court. Expect the next shot to be a weak one that you can attack.

Drills: 6.5, 6.8, 6.9

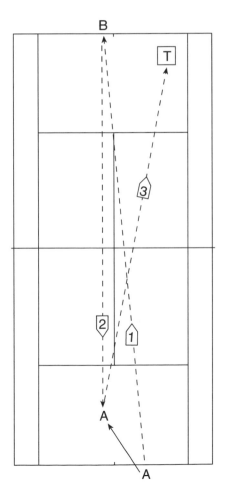

PATTERN **23**

From a Ball in Left Half of the Court
Drive Inside-Out Off the Court

Objective: If your opponent hits down the line from his forehand corner, step around the shot and drive an inside-out forehand that pulls him off the court.

Drills: 6.5, 6.8

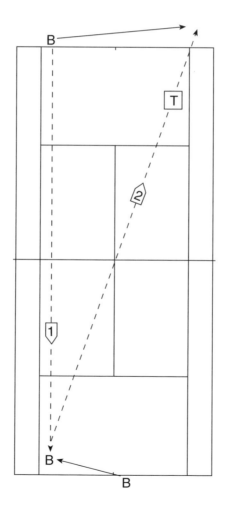

PATTERN **24**

When Driven Deep

Hit Looping Drives to Opponent's Backhand

Objective: Hit a looping drive to your opponent's backhand (especially against a one-hander) and look for a short ball to take out of the air or hit a winner after the bounce.

Drills: 6.5, 6.10

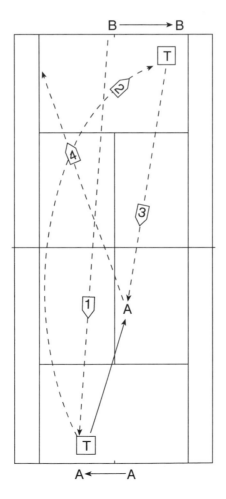

PATTERN **25**

Exchange Sliced Backhands

Attack a Short Ball

Objective: Keep your opponent deep until you get a short ball that you can attack.

Drills: 6.5, 6.12

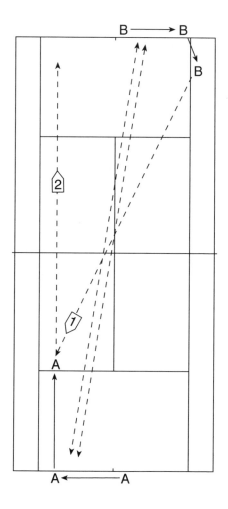

PATTERN **26**

Against Deep Shots in the Middle

Hit High and Deep Down the Middle

Objective: Reduce your opponent's angles and avoid errors by hitting high and deep down the middle of the court.

Drills: 6.5, 6.11

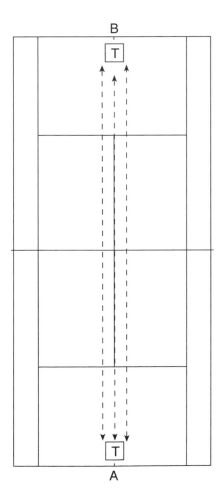

 *Chapter 6*

Groundstroke Drills

The first two drills in this chapter set the stage by emphasizing steadiness and control from the backcourt. As you improve your control and add depth to your shots, drills 6.3, 6.4, 6.5, and 6.6 show you how to take charge of the point. At higher levels of play, you'll want to perfect the shots in drills 6.7 through 6.12, especially if you are an aggressive baseliner. Andre Agassi and Monica Seles are masters of these patterns, and they love to punish opponents with their groundstrokes.

DRILL **6.1**

Crosscourt Rally Competition

Patterns

19 - 21

Category: *Groundstrokes*

Purpose: To practice crosscourt forehands and backhands emphasizing consistency and depth.

Equipment: Ropes or chalk to outline target areas.

Level: Beginner to professional.

Time: Play until one team scores 21 points.

Procedure: Player A begins the rally with a drop and hit to player C, and players rally crosscourt forehands. Each player scores a point for balls that land in the target areas. Players B and D replicate the drill at the same time using backhands. The first pair that scores 21 points is the winner. Players then switch sides of the court to hit the opposite stroke.

Coaching Points:

- Stress good net clearance for consistency and depth.
- Be sure to move back to the starting position after each groundstroke, as you would in a match, rather than standing in one spot.

DRILL **6.1**

Crosscourt Rally Competition

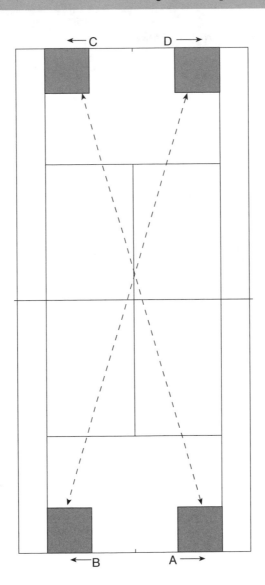

Patterns

19 - 21

DRILL **6.2**

 Alley Rally for Time

Pattern

19

Category: *Groundstrokes*

Purpose: To develop consistency and accuracy on forehand and backhand drives.

Equipment: None.

Level: Advanced beginner to professional.

Time: 10 minutes total.

Procedure: Player A hits forehands only to player D's backhand and they continue the rally. Any ball that lands in the alley scores a point for the team of players A and D. Players B and C replicate the drill on the other side of the court and keep their own team score. After 5 minutes of play, the team with the most successful shots landing in the alley wins the game. The teams switch sides of the court to begin the next game.

Coaching Points:

- Emphasize proper technique, early preparation, and footwork.
- Stress hitting through the shot with good balance.

DRILL **6.2**

Alley Rally for Time

Pattern

19

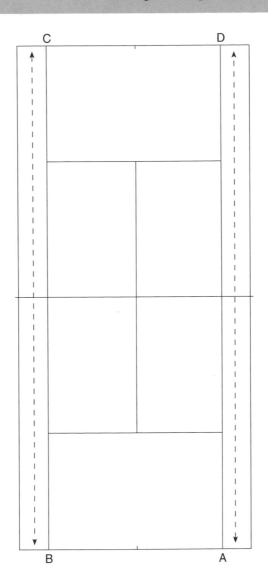

DRILL **6.3**

 Dictate and React

Patterns

19 - 21

Category: *Groundstrokes*

Purpose: To develop efficient movement, court coverage, consistency, and placement of groundstrokes.

Equipment: None.

Level: Advanced beginner to professional.

Time: Approximately 20 minutes.

Procedure: Player A puts the ball in play and dictates the rally by varying shots to all areas of the backcourt. Player B returns every ball to the shaded area or deep quadrant of player A's backcourt. After 5 minutes, players reverse roles. Then repeat the drill on the other half of the court.

Coaching Points:

- The "dictator" should stress consistency, variety of spins, and speed.
- The "reactor" should work on court coverage, consistency, and depth.

Dictate and React

Patterns

19 - 21

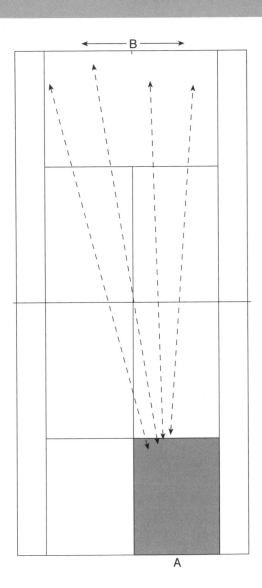

DRILL **6.4**

 Agassi

Pattern

19

Category: *Groundstrokes*

Purpose: To develop steadiness crosscourt to set up a forcing shot down the line.

Equipment: Targets of hoops, cones, or disks.

Level: Intermediate to professional.

Time: A total of 20 minutes for all variations.

Procedure: Players A and B rally crosscourt for four to six balls. Player B then hits a relatively weak, short ball so that player A can attack with a drive down the line to the target for a winner.

Variation:

1. Switch the roles of players A and B.
2. Repeat the drill on the other half of the court.

Coaching Points:

- Stress consistency and depth during the rally.
- On the winning shot down the line, players should move forward and hit the shot relatively flat.

DRILL **6.4**

Agassi

B

Pattern

19

DRILL **6.5**

 Partner Deep Game

Patterns

19 - 26

Category: *Groundstrokes*

Purpose: To develop consistency, depth, and placement on groundstrokes.

Equipment: None.

Level: Beginner to intermediate.

Time: Play until one team scores 21 points.

Procedure: Player A begins the point with a drop and hit to start the rally. Players A and C exchange groundstrokes that must land beyond the service line into the shaded area of the court. If player A loses the point, she is replaced by teammate B, who plays the next point against player C. If player C loses a point, she is replaced by teammate D. The winning team must earn 21 points and win by at least 2 points. After a total of 5 points, 10 points, and so on, the opposite team begins the rally.

Coaching Point:

- Players should work on steadiness and height over the net and use a variety of spins and speed.

DRILL **6.5**

Partner Deep Game

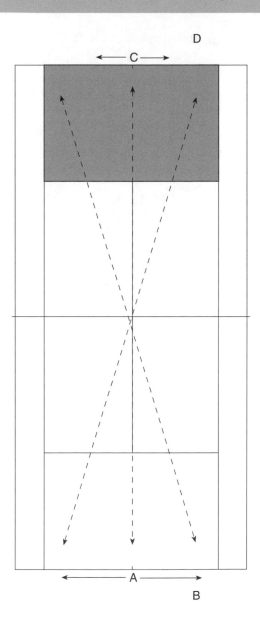

DRILL **6.6**

 Choose Your Winner

Patterns

19 and 20

Category: *Groundstrokes*

Purpose: To practice a winning drive from a short ball.

Equipment: Targets of hoops, cones, or disks.

Level: Intermediate to advanced.

Time: After 5 minutes, players switch roles. When both players have had a turn, repeat the drill on the opposite side of the court.

Procedure: Players A and B rally crosscourt for four to six balls. Player B hits a short ball to the *outside third* of the court. Player A has the option of hitting a winner down the line or through the court crosscourt. Player A earns a point each time his attempted winning shot is not returned into the court by player B.

Coaching Points:

- Player A must drive the ball aggressively through the court.
- Emphasize identical preparation for every shot to disguise the direction of the winning shot attempt.

Choose Your Winner

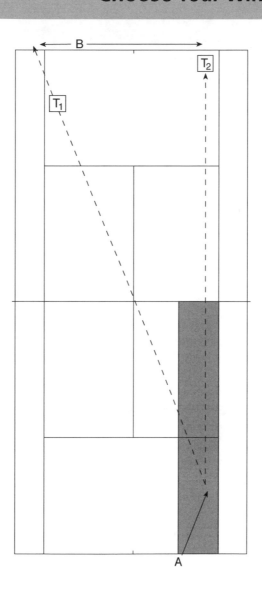

Patterns

19 and 20

DRILL **6.7**

Opening the Court With a Groundstroke

Pattern

21

Category: *Groundstrokes*

Purpose: To learn to open up the court with a severely angled groundstroke.

Equipment: A target of cones, hoops, or disks.

Level: Intermediate to advanced.

Time: Play until player A is successful five times, then switch roles.

Procedure: Players A and B rally crosscourt for four to six balls. Player B hits a short ball very wide to the *outside third* of the court. Player A replies with a severely angled, heavy topspin crosscourt shot that draws player B off the court. Player A drives his next shot aggressively to the open court for a winner. After both players have had a turn hitting winning shots, repeat the drill on the opposite side of the court.

Coaching Point:

- Be sure to emphasize the speed of the racquet head upward to impart heavy topspin on the severely angled crosscourt shot.

Opening the Court With a Groundstroke

Pattern

21

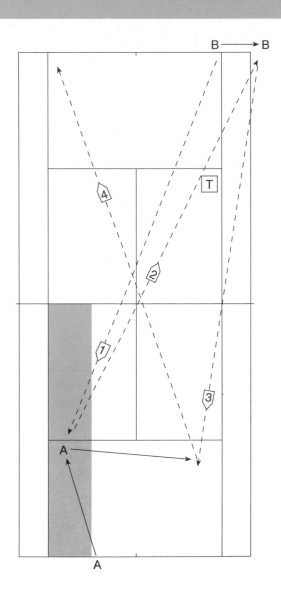

DRILL **6.8**

 Inside-Out Forehand

Patterns

22 and 23

Category: *Groundstrokes*

Purpose: To practice the technique of the inside-out forehand and make decisions whether to aim deep through the court or aim for the sharper angle off the court.

Equipment: Targets of hoops, cones, or disks.

Level: Intermediate to professional.

Time: 20 to 30 minutes.

Procedure: A coach feeds the ball to player A, who executes an inside-out forehand aiming for either target T_1 or target T_2. The player decides which target to aim for based on his position in the court relative to the oncoming ball. This is a dead-ball drill that should be used for players who are in the early stages of learning the inside-out shot. Eventually this shot may become an effective weapon.

Coaching Points:

- Emphasize quick movement into position, good shoulder turn, and balance.
- Players should contact the ball on the rise and get their body weight into the shot.

DRILL **6.8**

Inside-Out Forehand

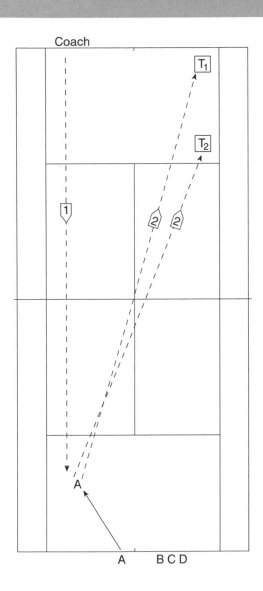

Coach

Patterns

22 and 23

DRILL **6.9**

Inside-Out Forehand Rally

Pattern

22

Category: *Groundstrokes*

Purpose: To develop consistency of the inside-out forehand to set up a winning forehand drive.

Equipment: Targets of cones, disks, or towels.

Level: Intermediate to professional.

Time: All players should get about 15 minutes of practice hitting the winning shots.

Procedure: Players A and B rally inside-out forehands to the shaded areas of the court. After an exchange of several hits, player B should hit a short ball that allows player A to go for a winning shot by hitting an inside-out forehand off the court or down the sideline to the target. Player B is not allowed to go for a winning shot. If player A misses a shot, player C replaces her and player D follows in turn. Every few minutes, one of the other players should replace B.

Coaching Points:

- Player B should work on consistency and may be allowed to hit either forehands or backhands.
- Players A, C, and D are aiming to develop the forehand as a weapon.

DRILL **6.9**

Inside-Out Forehand Rally

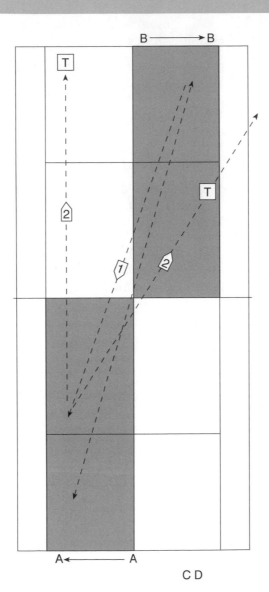

DRILL **6.10**

High Looping Drives

Pattern
24

Category: *Groundstrokes*

Purpose: To practice hitting high looping drives to an opponent's backhand side.

Equipment: A rope stretched across the court at a height four feet above the net.

Level: Intermediate to professional.

Time: After one trial, players C and D replace players A and B. After 10 minutes, switch the attacking and defending teams.

Procedure: Players A and B exchange high looping drives, aiming for the shaded areas of the court. After a rally of four to six balls, player A must move inside the baseline and take player B's shot out of the air. Player A should aim for a winning volley to target T_2.

Coaching Points:

- Both players should aim looping drives above the rope.
- Players should control the depth of their drives by applying heavy topspin using racquet head acceleration upward through the hitting area.

DRILL **6.10**

High Looping Drives

Pattern

24

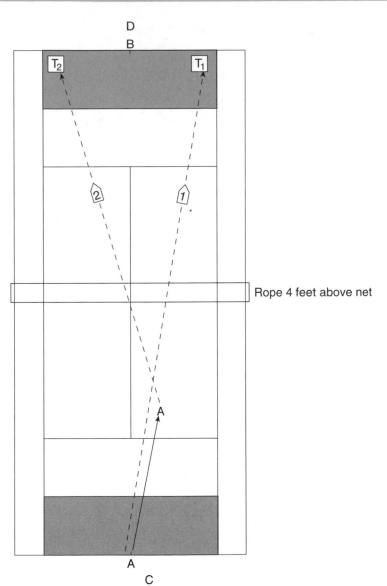

Rope 4 feet above net

DRILL **6.11**

 Defending Your Turf

Pattern

26

Category: *Groundstrokes*

Purpose: To defend against shots that land deep in the center third of your court.

Equipment: A rope stretched four feet above the net; ropes or chalk lines to outline shaded areas of the court.

Level: Beginner to professional.

Time: 15 to 20 minutes.

Procedure: Player A begins the rally with a drop and hit to player B. Players rally deep down the middle, aiming to clear the rope stretched over the net. Any ball that lands outside the shaded area of the court scores a point for the opponent. After 5 points are played, player B begins the next point. The first player to score 11 points wins the game. Players change ends of the court for the next game.

Variation: After players develop some skill with this pattern, vary it by allowing one or either player to move in, take the ball out of the air, and try to end the point at the net.

Coaching Points:

- Emphasize clearing the rope on every shot to ensure a good margin of safety and depth.
- Point out the advantage of a deep defensive shot down the middle of the court that provides no angles for the opponent.

Defending Your Turf

Pattern

26

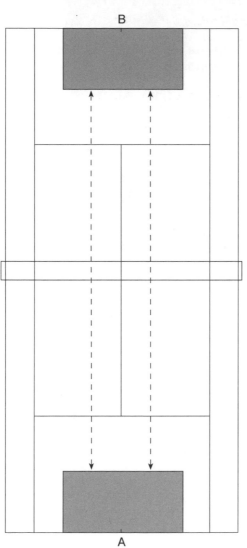

Rope 4 feet above net

DRILL **6.12**

 Slice and Dice

Pattern

25

Category: *Groundstrokes*

Purpose: To develop the slice backhand, keep the bounce low, and move your opponent.

Equipment: Targets of cones, hoops, or disks.

Level: Intermediate to professional.

Time: Rotate every 3 to 5 minutes, as player D may do a lot of running.

Procedure: Player D begins the rally by hitting to the shaded area of the court (player A's backhand). Player A continues the rally by hitting *only* slice backhands to any of the four targets as shown until the point is played out. Then player B replaces player A. Be sure that player D hits every ball to the shaded area of the court.

Coaching Points:

- Encourage players A, B, and C to aim most of their shots to targets T_1 or T_2 to open the court for an aggressive shot to T_3.
- Allow players to attempt an occasional drop shot to T_4, but caution them to disguise it well by using the identical preparation used for the slice backhand.

DRILL **6.12**

Slice and Dice

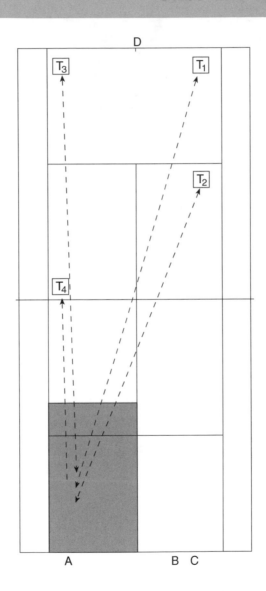

PART III

Midcourt
Patterns and Drills

Balls that land in the midcourt are an invitation for you to shift from playing defensively to attacking by hitting a forcing drive, a winner, or an approach shot. Seize control of the point and make something positive happen. At the same time, use controlled aggression because you are not quite in a position of dominance, as you are when you reach the net.

The patterns in chapter 7 and drills in chapter 8 will help you understand the strategy and skills from the midcourt. Any ball from your opponent that lands short should immediately trigger an attack by you. Look for the opportunity beginning with weak second serves from your opponent; they are simply short balls that are begging to be exploited.

Chapter 7

Midcourt Patterns

From the midcourt, the laws of physics dictate that the flight of the ball from your racquet must be straight to keep it within the court. *Most* of your shots should be directed down the line, and you should follow the path of the ball to the net. This will allow you to bisect the angle of possible returns by keeping you on the same side of the court as the ball. If you hit crosscourt and follow it in, you have to move across the centerline to bisect the angle of returns. That will take more time and allow more angles for your opponent to pass you at the net.

The technique of midcourt shots is different from backcourt ones in that you should probably shorten your backswing to compensate for the forward movement of your body and the reduced distance the ball must travel. Unlike baseline shots, where you should firmly plant your feet before the shot, midcourt shots are hit on the move toward the net. Footwork and balance are critical to ensure a smooth transition through the midcourt.

Use backspin or topspin on most shots to control the depth of your shots. When you go for a winning drive, flatten the shot by applying less spin to drive the ball through the court. Be sure to prepare the same way whether hitting a drive, an approach shot, or a drop shot so that your opponent cannot anticipate your choice of shots.

You should go for a winning drive from the midcourt when you can contact the ball at the height of the net or above. Be sure you are balanced and prepared early to hit the shot. If you must contact the ball below the level of the net, your best option is to slice an approach shot and follow it to the net.

The drop shot is an enticing option from the midcourt, but it has relatively high risk, particularly on hard courts. It is also a poor choice in pressure situations because it requires a delicate touch. Drop shots with the wind at your back are also risky because the ball will carry too deep into the court.

The eight patterns presented in this chapter reflect this high-percentage midcourt strategy. Use the drills in chapter 8 to reinforce the patterns you find here.

PATTERN **27**

If Ball Is Above the Net
Drive Hard and Flat Down the Line

Objective: Follow your shot to the net and volley the next ball to the open court.

Drills: 8.1, 8.2, 8.5, 8.9, 8.10, 8.11

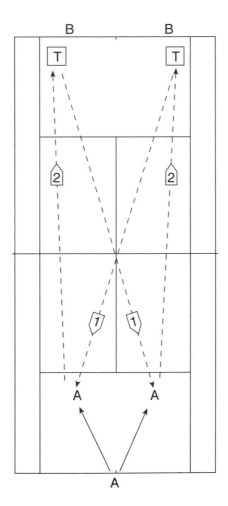

PATTERN **28**

If Ball Is Above the Net

Drive Crosscourt for a Winner

Objective: Use this pattern as a variation of pattern 27 to prevent your opponent from anticipating your shot down the line.

Drills: 8.10, 8.11

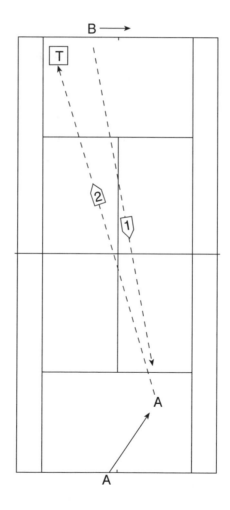

PATTERN **29**

| If Ball Is Below the Net |
| *Slice Down the Line* |

Objective: Use the safety of the sliced approach shot by opening the racquet face and hitting through the shot to achieve good depth. Follow the ball to the net and volley the next shot to the open court.

Drills: 8.1, 8.2, 8.3, 8.5, 8.9, 8.10, 8.11

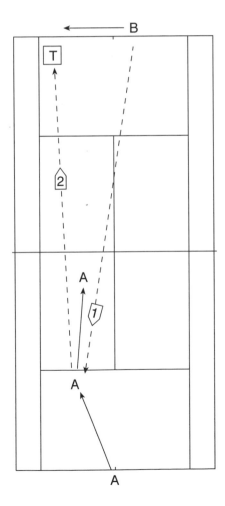

PATTERN **30**

If Ball Is Below the Net
Drop Shot Down the Line

Objective: Use the drop shot as a variation of pattern 29 to keep your opponent off balance.

Drills: 8.4, 8.10, 8.11

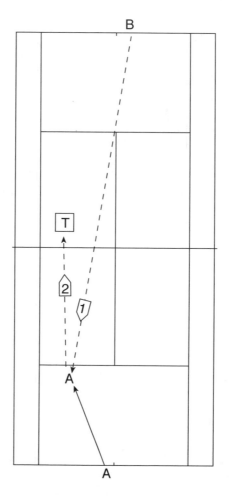

PATTERN **31**

From a Ball in the Middle

Approach Down the Middle

Objective: Approach down the middle to reduce the angle of possible returns.

Drills: 8.6, 8.10, 8.11

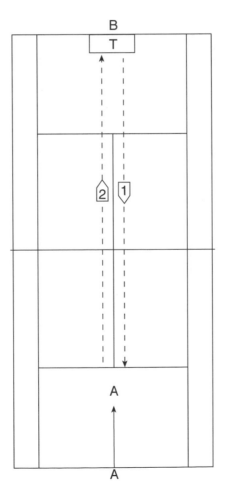

PATTERN **32**

From a Ball in the Middle

Use an Inside-Out Forehand Approach

Objective: If your forehand is your strongest shot, run around your backhand to use the inside-out forehand for the approach shot.

Drills: 8.7, 8.10, 8.11

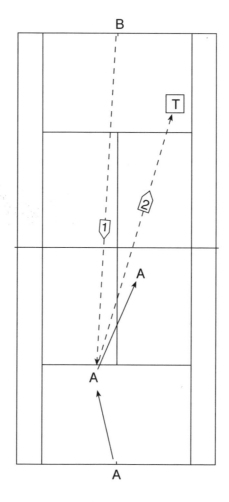

PATTERN **33**

From a Deep, High-Bouncing Shot

Use a Looping Topspin Approach

Objective: Loop a heavy topspin shot deep to your opponent's weaker side, which is often the backhand.

Drills: 8.8, 8.10, 8.11

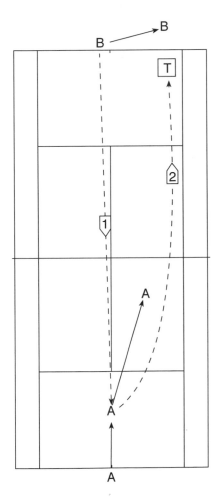

PATTERN **34**

From a Looped Shot
Move In and Hit an Approach Volley

Objective: When your opponent is pulled wide and tries to recover position by looping a shot, move in to hit an approach volley out of the air. For one-handers, this is typically a sliced shot, whereas two-handers may drive the volley.

Drill: 8.12

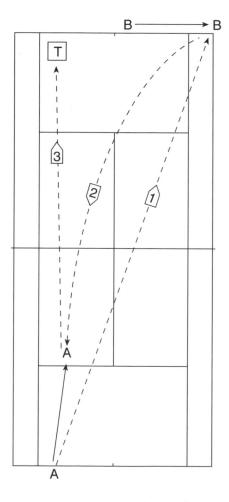

 **Chapter 8**

Midcourt Drills

Once you get a short ball in the midcourt, you've got a green light to attack. Your decision should be automatic, and if you can contact the ball above the net, you should deliver a punishing shot.

The first several drills will help you refine the *technique* of midcourt shots and learn to make the right shot selection. As your skills and decision making improve, you'll enjoy the challenge of drills 8.9, 8.10, and 8.11, which replicate the continuous action of playing points.

Check your progress in midcourt play using the Weak Serve drill (8.11). If you don't win every game against a weak serve, there's more work to be done on your midcourt skills.

DRILL **8.1**

 Approach to Targets

Patterns

27 and 29

Category: *Midcourt*

Purpose: To practice the technique of the approach shot.

Equipment: Targets of hoops, cones, or disks; a hopper of balls.

Level: Beginner to advanced.

Time: 15 to 20 minutes.

Procedure: Players form two lines on either side of the court with the first player in each line at three-quarter court. The coach feeds a short ball alternately to the lines on the left and right. The first player hits an approach shot down the line to the target and rotates to the opposite line. Players should hit forehands or backhands on the appropriate side of the court.

Coaching Points:

- The feeds should come rapidly so that players get the maximum number of trials in a short period.
- Two players should be designated as retrievers to replenish the ball supply.
- This drill provides time to work on the technique of the shot; thus the coach may wish to have players feed so that he can be on the same side of the net as the hitters.

DRILL **8.1**

Approach to Targets

Patterns

27 and 29

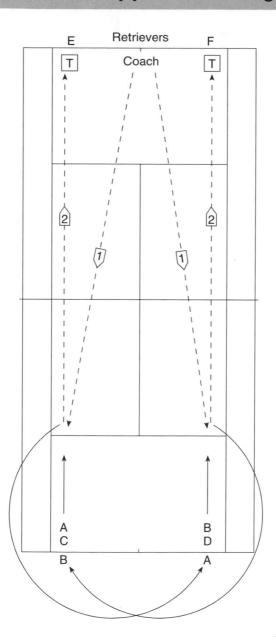

DRILL **8.2**

 One- or Two-Handed Approach

Patterns

27 and 29

Category: *Midcourt*

Purpose: To practice making the decision whether to use one or two hands on the backhand approach shot.

Equipment: Targets of hoops, cones, or disks; a hopper of balls.

Level: Intermediate to professional.

Time: 15 minutes.

Procedure: The coach feeds a ball to player A, who hits it down the line. The next shot is short crosscourt to the backhand side. If the ball is near the center third of the court and bounces at the height of the net or above, player A should drive it with two hands. If the ball is wide to the outside of the court or bounces low, he should hit a one-handed slice approach toward the target down the line. After player A completes the sequence, player B takes his turn.

Coaching Points:

- To encourage early recognition of the shot, players should call out "one" or "two" as early as they can.
- When players are successful on the approach shots, add a winning volley to complete the point.

DRILL **8.2**

One- or Two-Handed Approach

Patterns

27 and 29

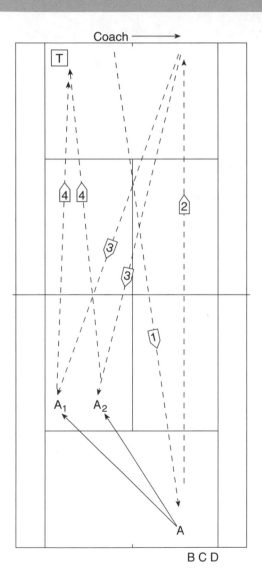

DRILL **8.3**

Backhand Slice Approach With Carioca Step

Pattern

29

Category: *Midcourt*

Purpose: To learn the proper footwork on the backhand approach shot.

Equipment: A hopper of balls and target.

Level: Beginner to advanced.

Time: 15 minutes.

Procedure: Player A moves forward, expecting a short ball on the backhand side, and faces the net. As the ball bounces, he moves the right foot forward and plants it as he turns sideways and prepares the racquet. The left foot then drops behind his body as the ball is struck. During contact with the ball, he keeps the shoulders sideways by throwing the free arm backward toward the fence. After the shot, he squares around and continues toward the net to prepare for a volley.

Coaching Points:

- When players are successful, have them start at the baseline and move up to the ball.
- To move to a live-ball drill, the coach should feed a ball to the forehand side before hitting a short ball. At this stage, you can add the finishing volley crosscourt to end the point.

DRILL **8.3**

Backhand Slice Approach With Carioca Step

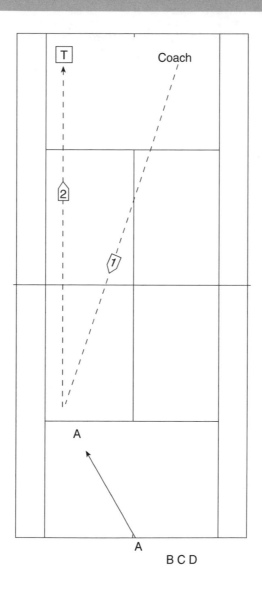

DRILL 8.4

 Backhand Slice—Drop Shot Variation

Pattern

30

Category: *Midcourt*

Purpose: To practice a backhand drop shot as a variation of the approach.

Equipment: A hopper of balls and target.

Level: Intermediate to advanced.

Time: 15 minutes.

Procedure: Player D begins the point to player A's forehand. Player A drives the ball down the line and player D returns it short crosscourt. Player A attempts a drop shot to T_1 and is then replaced by player B for her turn.

After approximately 5 minutes, change the drill by having player D call out just before the hit whether the players should aim a drop shot for target T_1 or an approach to T_2.

Coaching Points:

- Emphasize disguise in the preparation for the shot.
- After players gain some skill with the sequence, you can begin to keep track of the number of successful shots made.

Backhand Slice—Drop Shot Variation

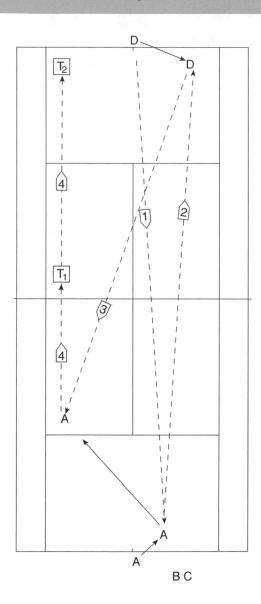

DRILL **8.5**

 Approach—High or Low Bounce

Patterns

27 and 29

Category: *Midcourt*

Purpose: To help players recognize the correct shot depending on the bounce of the ball.

Equipment: Targets in the deep corners.

Level: Intermediate to professional.

Time: 15 minutes.

Procedure: Players A and B begin by rallying four to six balls crosscourt. Player B then hits a short ball to player A, who decides whether to drive or slice the ball based on the height of the ball at contact. He must also decide whether to hit the shot down the line or go for a winner crosscourt. In general, balls that can be taken at the height of the net or above should be driven, and balls below the net should be sliced down the line.

Variation: Have players replicate the drill on the backhand side.

Coaching Points:

- After both players have had a turn hitting the approach shots, play the points out to conclusion and keep score.
- Remind players to disguise their shot as they prepare the racquet so that their opponent is uncertain.

DRILL **8.5**

Approach—High or Low Bounce

Patterns

**27 and
29**

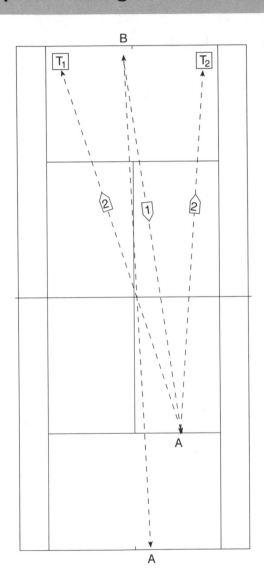

DRILL **8.6**

Down-the-Middle Approach

Pattern

31

Category: *Midcourt*

Purpose: To practice the approach shot down the middle and reduce the angle of possible passing shots.

Equipment: Targets of hoops, cones, or disks.

Level: Beginner to advanced.

Time: 10 to 15 minutes.

Procedure: Players A and B rally down the middle until player B hits a ball that lands around the "T" of the service lines. Player A moves forward and hits either a forehand or backhand approach shot deep down the middle, aiming for target T_1, and closes in to the net. Player B replies with a passing shot to either side, which player A volleys crosscourt for a winner.

Variation: Additional players can be added to the drill and points awarded for successful trials using a team format.

Coaching Points:

- The approach shot down the middle should be used when your opponent has demonstrated good passing shots from the corners.
- Be sure to aim deep on this shot to drive your opponent back and reduce the angle for passing shots as much as possible.

DRILL **8.6**

Down-the-Middle Approach

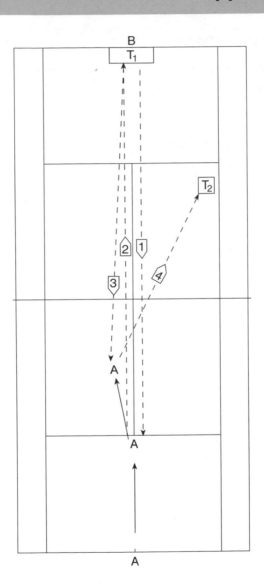

DRILL **8.7**

 ## Inside-Out Forehand Approach

Pattern

32

Category: *Midcourt*

Purpose: To learn how to use the forehand drive as a weapon for the approach shot.

Equipment: A hopper of balls and target.

Level: Intermediate to professional.

Time: 10 to 15 minutes.

Procedure: Players A and B rally several balls until player B hits a shot that lands around the service line on the ad court. Player A moves quickly around the ball and hits an inside-out forehand drive toward the target, forcing player B off the court. Player B tries a passing shot, and they play out the point.

Variation: Additional players can be added to the drill and points awarded for successful trials using a team format.
  After 5 to 10 minutes, have players A and B switch roles.

Coaching Points:

- Urge players to recognize the short ball early so they have time to move around the shot and establish good balance.
- Stress hitting the ball at the peak of the bounce or on the rise and driving the ball aggressively at the target.

Inside-Out Forehand Approach

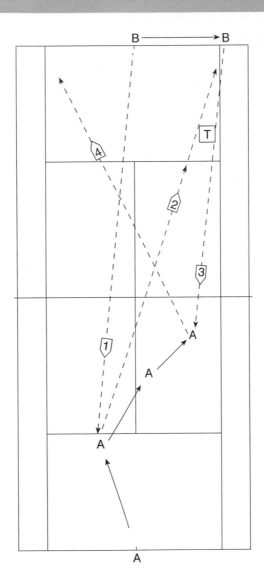

Pattern

32

DRILL **8.8**

Loop Approach

Pattern

33

Category: *Midcourt*

Purpose: To practice looping the approach shot against an opponent playing deep behind the baseline.

Equipment: Target of hoops, cones, or disks; a rope stretched across the net.

Level: Beginner to professional.

Time: 10 minutes.

Procedure: Players A and B rally four to six balls deep crosscourt until player A gets a ball to hit with a looping topspin shot deep to the target. As player B tries a passing shot, player A moves in and volleys the ball away for a winner.

Coaching Points:

- Be sure the looping approach shot clears the net and has plenty of topspin to control the depth and moves forward after the bounce. The racquet should accelerate sharply upward to achieve maximum topspin.
- As player A moves in to volley, stress a split-step for balance and to defend against a possible lob return.

DRILL **8.8**

Loop Approach

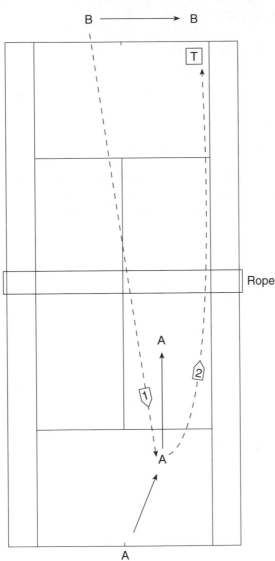

Rope 6 feet above net

DRILL **8.9**

Continuous Approach

Patterns

27 and 29

Category: *Midcourt*

Purpose: To develop control and rhythm of the baseline rally followed by an approach and volley.

Equipment: A hopper of balls on each side of the net.

Level: Intermediate to advanced.

Time: 20 minutes.

Procedure: Two players form a team on each side of the net at the baseline. Player A begins the drill with a crosscourt forehand to player C, who returns short to the forehand of player A. Player A hits an approach shot to player C's backhand, and player C hits a passing shot down the line. Player A volleys the ball crosscourt to player D, who keeps the ball in play crosscourt and then repeats the sequence with player B as his partner. After some success is achieved, switch roles of the teams and repeat the drill for both teams on the backhand.

Coaching Points:

- Players should be encouraged to hit the ball at about three-quarter speed in the beginning of the drill to gain control.
- Each player should have an extra ball or two in his pocket so that if he misses a shot, he can quickly put another ball in play from the same spot and maintain the rhythm of the drill.

DRILL **8.9**

Continuous Approach

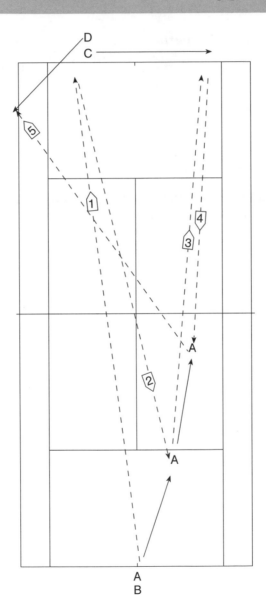

DRILL **8.10**

 Partner "21"

Patterns

27 - 33

Category: *Midcourt*

Purpose: To play a competitive game that encompasses practice on all the midcourt shots.

Equipment: None.

Level: Intermediate to professional.

Time: 15 to 30 minutes.

Procedure: Players A and B compete as a team against players C and D. The play begins with player A putting the ball in play to player C, with both players at their respective baselines. The two players rally until one receives a short ball to attack. The attacking player may choose to hit an approach shot, a drop shot, or a winning drive, and the point is played out. The player who loses the point is replaced by her partner for the next point. If an error occurs during the beginning rally, no points are awarded to either team and the point is replayed.

After 5 points, 10 points, and so on, the other team puts the ball in play to begin the point. The winning team must accumulate 21 points and win by at least 2 points.

Coaching Points:

- To assess player skill and strategy, the coach should let players experiment with all the shots that can be hit from the midcourt.
- Specific comments on choice of shots or technique should be made while partners are waiting their turn.

Partner "21"

Patterns

27 - 33

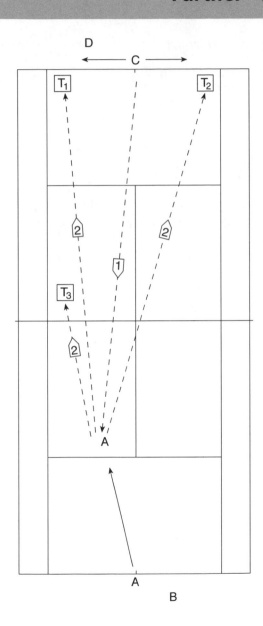

DRILL **8.11**

 Weak Serve

Patterns

27 - 33

Category: *Midcourt*

Purpose: To test your ability to execute midcourt shots and attack a weak serve.

Equipment: None.

Level: Intermediate to professional.

Time: 20 to 30 minutes.

Procedure: Two players compete in a regular set with normal scoring except that the server (A) gets only one serve that must be played underhand out of his hand and below waist level. The receiver (B) must play the ball with his forehand on the deuce court if he is right-handed and with his backhand on the ad court.

The receiver must hit the return and rush the net for the next shot or lose the point. Naturally, he should try a mixture of approach shots, winning drives, and drop shots.

Coaching Points:

- This game will quickly reveal weaknesses in the transition game and in a player's ability to attack a weak serve. You should expect players to lose their serve every time.
- Point out to players the carryover to actual match play when they should look for opportunities to attack a weak second serve.

Weak Serve

Patterns

27 - 33

DRILL **8.12**

 Sneak Attack—Approach Volley

Pattern

34

Category: *Midcourt*

Purpose: To learn how and when to sneak in to the net by taking an approach volley out of the air.

Equipment: None.

Level: Intermediate to professional.

Time: 10 to 15 minutes.

Procedure: Player A feeds an aggressive deep shot that puts player B on the defensive and off the court. When player B replies with a high looping shot to gain time to recover position, player A sneaks into the midcourt and takes the ball out of the air with a volley down the line. The point is played out to its conclusion. If more players are involved in the drill, they can rotate into the play, and score can be kept of the number of successful attempts.

Coaching Points:

- Good balance and timing of the split-step are critical for the player moving forward.
- Because the volley is made farther from the net than normal, the follow-through should be level and a bit longer than usual.
- Two-handers will probably be more comfortable with a two-handed volley on the backhand side.

DRILL **8.12**

Sneak Attack—Approach Volley

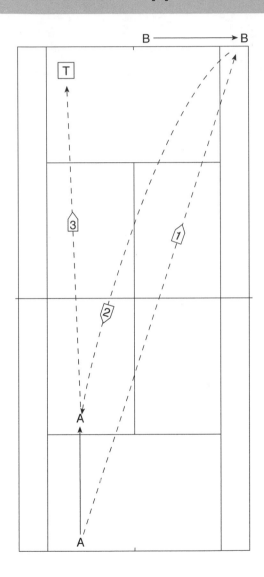

Pattern

34

 *PART IV*

Net Play Patterns and Drills

Getting to the net can be the most exciting part of tennis. You are clearly in the driver's seat and have the opportunity to win the point. Because you are closer to your opponent than you were in the backcourt, the ball will reach you sooner, and the type of shot you hit will require very little backswing.

The patterns in chapter 9 and the drills in chapter 10 will prepare you for the situations that typically occur when you reach the net. Many of the drills combine several shots, because play at the net usually occurs as the point develops. Several drills are designed to practice the serve-and-volley technique, which is rather advanced and certainly used by more players in their doubles play than in singles.

Chapter 9

Net Play Patterns

Winning net play depends on solid volleys and overheads.

Volleys are hit with a short, compact movement that begins with a shoulder turn to prepare the racquet and continues with a short move forward to align the racquet face with the oncoming ball. As your opponent strikes the ball, split-step to establish your balance and then close in quickly to volley or retreat to hit an overhead smash. Closing in makes it difficult for your opponent to pass you and opens up more angles for winning volleys. Whenever possible, move forward on a diagonal to close off the possible angles rather than simply moving sideways to get to the ball. Your objective is to work your way close enough to the net that you can direct the ball downward into the court. Keep your upper body relatively straight and bend from the knees on low volleys. Good balance is essential at the net to allow quick recovery for the next shot.

The overhead smash is the single most spectacular shot in tennis and should end the point in your favor. The technique is similar to the serve, but because you are closer to the net and trying to direct the ball downward, the contact point should be well in front of your body. The racquet face at contact will cause the ball to go down into the court, so you must be sure to keep your head and chin up throughout the hit to avoid pulling the ball downward too quickly.

The patterns in this chapter reinforce the following net play strategies:

- Balls that you can hit above the net should generally be directed crosscourt and deep to the open court or, if you are close to the net, can be angled sharply crosscourt.
- Balls that you must hit below the net should be played safely deep down the line.

- If you hit the first volley from near your service line, the down-the-line shot or one to your opponent's weaker side are the best choices.

All the hard work you put in from the backcourt and midcourt have prepared you for the opportunity to move to the net into an attacking position. Ending the point in your favor with a well-placed volley or a powerful smash is truly the most fun in tennis. Enjoy your practice of net play, as you've worked hard to get here.

PATTERN **35**

If Ball Is Above the Net
Volley to Opponent's Weakness

Objective: After hitting the first volley to a weakness (maybe backhand), move in and volley the next shot to the open court.

Drills: 10.1, 10.2, 10.5

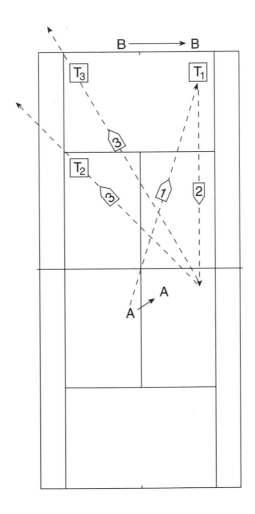

PATTERN **36**

If Ball Is Below the Net

Volley Deep Down the Line

Objective: Volley down the line to keep the ball in front of you and angle the next shot to the open court.

Drills: 10.1, 10.2, 10.3

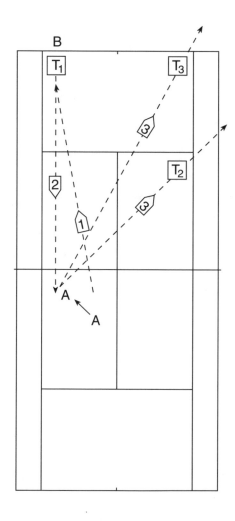

PATTERN 37

After Your Approach, if Ball Is Above the Net

Volley Deep Crosscourt

Objective: After your first volley, close in and volley the next shot short crosscourt on the opposite side for a winner.

Drills: 10.1, 10.2, 10.4

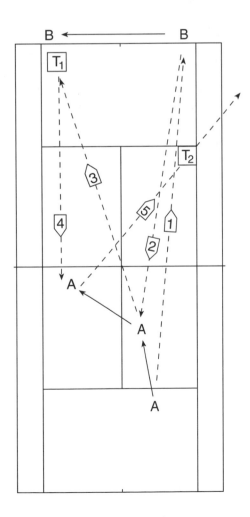

PATTERN **38**

Serve Wide and Volley to the Open Court

Objective: Pull the receiver wide with your serve and then hit your first volley to the open court on the opposite side.

Drills: 10.1, 10.6

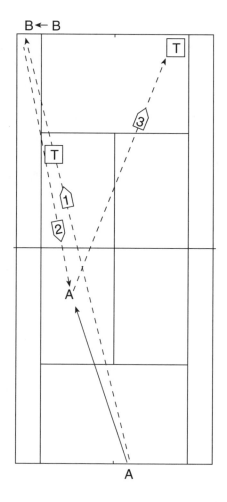

PATTERN **39**

Serve to the "T" and Volley Behind Opponent or to a Weakness

Objective: Pull the receiver to the middle with your serve and then volley behind her or to the weaker side.

Drills: 10.1, 10.7

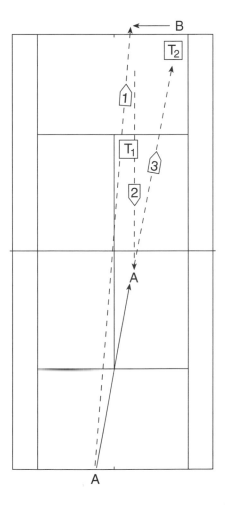

PATTERN 40

If Lob Is Short

Angle Your Overhead Away

Objective: Angle your overhead smash away or bounce it over the fence.

Drills: 10.8, 10.9, 10.10, 10.11, 10.14

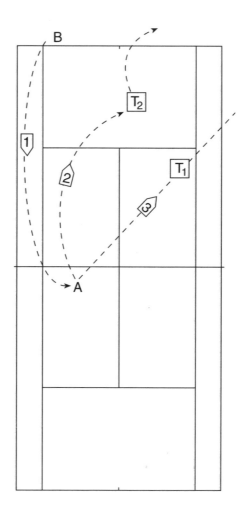

PATTERN **41**

If Lob Is Deep
Aim Your Overhead Crosscourt

Objective: Direct your overhead smash crosscourt and toward the middle for the best margin of error. After the smash, close in to the net in case your opponent returns your shot.

Drills: 10.9, 10.12, 10.14

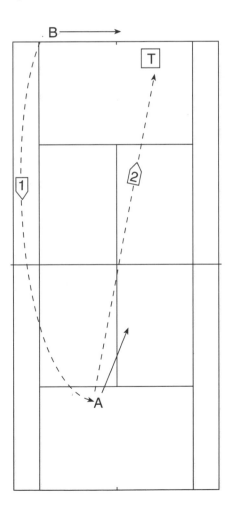

PATTERN 42

On High Lobs

Let Ball Bounce and Aim Crosscourt

Objective: If the lob is very high or complicated by the sun or wind, let the ball bounce and aim for the largest portion of the court. After the smash, close in to the net in case your opponent returns your shot.

Drills: 10.13, 10.14

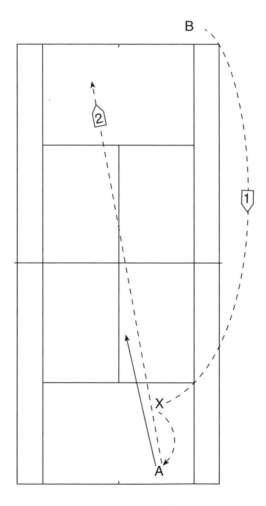

Chapter 10

Net Play Drills

For players who aspire to a serve-and-volley game, these drills are essential. Players like Stefan Edberg, Boris Becker, Martina Navratilova, and Pam Shriver have had great careers marked by thousands of trips to the net.

Even if you've chosen another style of play, these drills and skills will come in handy when you play doubles. If you coach, you should know that kids love these drills too, as no shots are more fun to hit than ones that end the point!

DRILL **10.1**

Volley to Targets

Patterns

35 - 39

Category: *Net Play*

Purpose: To develop technique and accuracy on eight possible volleys.

Equipment: Targets of hoops, cones, or disks.

Level: Beginner to advanced.

Time: 20 minutes.

Procedure: Use a ball machine or a feeder to give each volleyer eight shots in a row. Begin with forehand volleys deep crosscourt and down the line (targets T_1 and T_2). Follow with short angled volleys to the short crosscourt angle and finally down the line (targets T_3 and T_4). Repeat the sequence using the backhand volley.

After player A has completed his turn, he goes to the other side of the net to retrieve the eight balls and returns them to the ball hopper or machine. Player B follows by executing the same sequence, followed by player C and then player D.

Coaching Points:

- Be sure that players move forward diagonally to volley each ball.
- Apply underspin to the volley to help control the depth.
- For short angled volleys, reduce the length of the backswing.

Volley to Targets

Patterns

35 - 39

T₁   T₂

T₃   T₄

A ← → A

A

B C D

DRILL **10.2**

 ## High Ball—Low Ball

Patterns

35 - 37

Category: *Net Play*

Purpose: To practice reacting to the height of the ball at contact with the proper shot down the line or to the open court.

Equipment: A hopper of balls.

Level: Beginner to advanced.

Time: 10 to 15 minutes.

Procedure: The coach feeds the ball to player A at the net. If the ball is above the net, player A closes quickly and angles it deep or short crosscourt. If the ball is below the net, she plays it back down the line and waits for the next ball. After trying a winning volley, the player goes to the end of the line and the next player takes a turn. After a few minutes, switch the drill to the other half of the court.

Coaching Points:

- Start players with several low or wide balls to practice making the defensive volley. When they get a high ball, they should pounce on it for the put-away.
- Remind players to split-step to recover their balance before each volley.

DRILL **10.2**

High Ball—Low Ball

Patterns

35 - 37

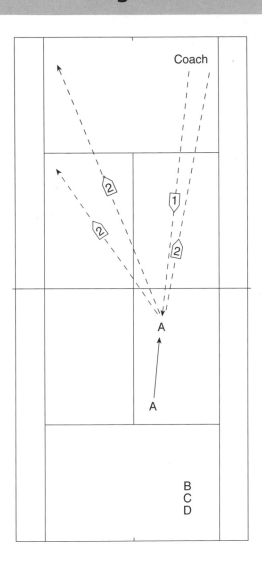

DRILL **10.3**

 Below the Net—Down the Line

Category: *Net Play*

Purpose: To develop the habit of volleying a low or wide ball deep down the line and angling the next volley away.

Equipment: Targets of hoops, cones, or disks.

Level: Beginner to advanced.

Time: 10 to 15 minutes.

Procedure: The coach feeds a ball low or wide to player A, who volleys it deep down the line to target T_1. The second ball is fed crosscourt and higher so that player A can close in to the net and angle it away for a winner to target T_2. The next player in line, player B, steps up for his turn. After a few minutes, switch the drill to the other half of the court.

Coaching Points:

- Be sure players keep their shoulders and back relatively straight and bend from the knees on low volleys. On wide balls, they should move diagonally toward the net to intercept the ball.
- Have players apply underspin to the ball to control the depth of their volleys.

DRILL **10.3**

Below the Net—Down the Line

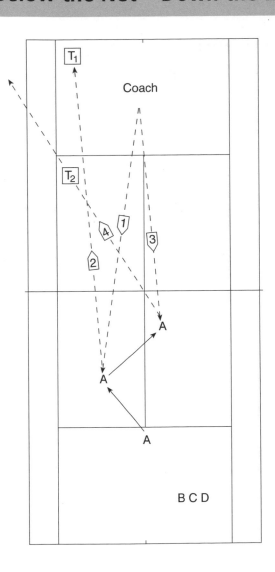

DRILL **10.4**

 ## Above the Net—To the Open Court

Category: *Net Play*

Purpose: To learn to follow an approach shot with a volley to the open court if the ball is above the net.

Equipment: Target of cones.

Level: Intermediate to professional.

Time: 20 minutes.

Procedure: The coach feeds a short ball to player A, who hits an approach shot down the line. The coach then hits a passing shot that player A can volley above the net and aim deep crosscourt to the target. Player C, who starts in the center of the baseline, moves over to play a passing shot down the line. Player A closes in toward the net diagonally and volleys the ball sharply for the short-angle winner. Players A and C are replaced by players B and D, who repeat the same pattern. After 10 minutes of drilling, switch the play to the other half of the court so that players learn the pattern on both the forehand and backhand sides.

Coaching Points:

- Check to see that players split-step before each volley to recover balance.
- Each player should have an extra ball available in case of an error so that she can put another ball in play from the same spot and continue the drill.

Above the Net—To the Open Court

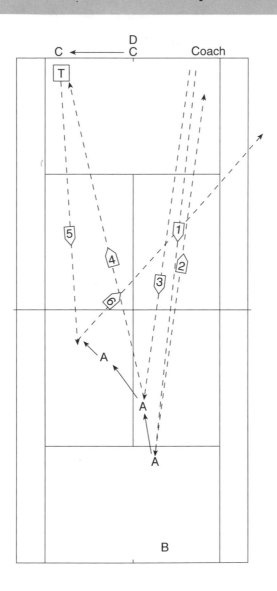

DRILL **10.5**

Above the Net—To a Weakness

Pattern

35

Category: *Net Play*

Purpose: To learn to follow an approach shot with a volley to the opponent's weakness if the ball is above the net.

Equipment: None.

Level: Intermediate to professional.

Time: 10 to 15 minutes.

Procedure: The coach feeds a short ball to player A, who hits an approach shot down the line. The coach then hits a crosscourt passing shot that player A can volley aggressively to the coach's weakness (backhand). The coach replies with a weak passing shot that player A can close out with a winning shot crosscourt. Player B then moves in for his turn. Players should keep track of the number of times they complete the pattern successfully. The first player to earn 10 successful trials is the winner.

After players achieve a reasonable degree of skill on one side of the court, repeat the drill on the other half of the court in case the weakness is on the forehand side or players face a left-hander with a weak backhand.

Coaching Points:

- Because players are attacking an opponent's weakness, insist on successful shots throughout the drill. Any missed shot causes them to lose their turn at that point.
- As a variation, the coach can hit a lob rather than a passing shot, because an opponent with a weaker side may elect that option. By mixing in the lob, players will be forced to react to the shot rather than closing in to the net too fast.

DRILL **10.5**

Above the Net—To a Weakness

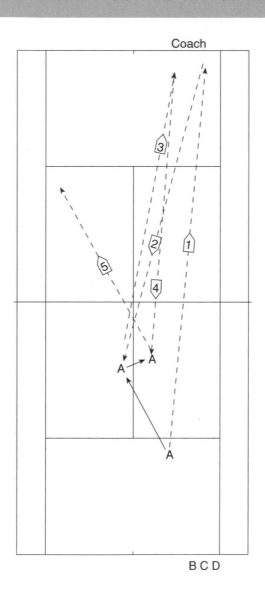

Coach

B C D

DRILL **10.6**

Serve Wide—Volley to the Open Court

Pattern

38

Category: *Net Play*

Purpose: To learn to open up the court with a wide serve and follow it to the net for a volley to the open court.

Equipment: Targets of hoops, cones, or disks.

Level: Intermediate to professional.

Time: 15 to 20 minutes.

Procedure: Player A begins the point with a wide serve that is sliced to the extreme outside indicated by target T_1. Player B returns the ball down the line so that player A can play the ball above the net. Player A, who has followed the serve in, split-steps just before B contacts the ball and then closes in to volley the ball deep to the open court, shown as target T_2. This is only a three-shot drill to emphasize the practice on the serve, return, and first volley.

As soon as players A and B have completed the sequence, players C and D repeat the same pattern on the other side of the court. In this case, the serve is kicked out wide to target T_3 and the volley is directed to target T_4.

Coaching Points:

- After the volley to the open court, players should follow the ball to get in the habit of covering the net correctly.
- Sometime during the drill, vary the return of serve by having it hit crosscourt. After players are successful with a predictable return, ask the receiver to mix up the returns with crosscourt or down-the-line shots.

DRILL **10.6**

Serve Wide—Volley to the Open Court

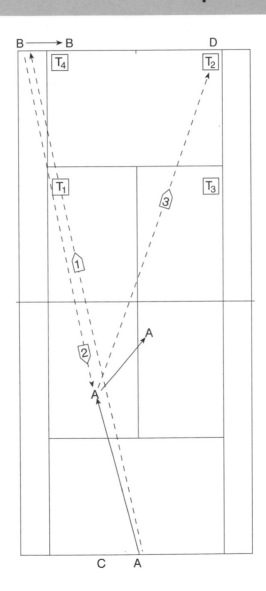

DRILL **10.7**

Serve to Middle—Volley Behind Opponent

Pattern

39

Category: *Net Play*

Purpose: To practice serving to the inside of the service box and hitting the first volley behind the opponent.

Equipment: Targets of hoops, cones, or disks.

Level: Intermediate to professional.

Time: 15 to 20 minutes.

Procedure: Player A begins the point with a serve to the inside corner of the ad service court indicated by target T_1 and follows the serve to the net. Player B returns the ball back down the middle of the court. After her split-step, Player A moves in and volleys the ball behind player B to target T_2. As soon as the sequence is completed, players C and D repeat the pattern on the other side of the court using targets T_3 and T_4.

During the drill, players should rotate sides of the court and change roles from server to receiver.

Coaching Points:

- If the server misses the serve, she loses her turn. If the receiver misses, she should put another ball in play out of her hand so that the server is not penalized.
- If players are competent on these first three shots, they can begin to play out the points to completion.

DRILL **10.7**

Serve to Middle—Volley Behind Opponent

Pattern

39

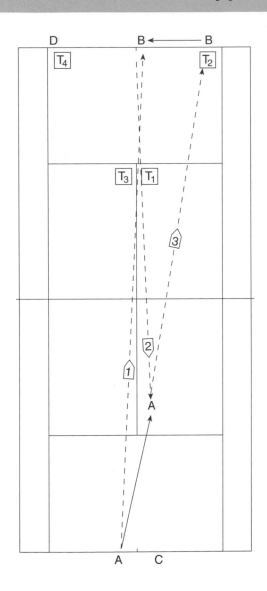

DRILL **10.8**

 Two Steps Up or Three Back

Pattern

40

Category: *Net Play*

Purpose: To practice moving up or back at the net.

Equipment: None.

Level: Beginner to advanced.

Time: 15 to 20 minutes.

Procedure: Players A, C, and E use half the court and players B, D, and F use the other half. Players must stay on their side of the centerline to prevent collisions.

The player at the net puts the ball in play underhand, and the baseline player either lobs or drives the ball, trying not to make an error. The net player moves two steps in before each volley or three steps back before each overhead smash, which is directed back to his baseline partner. The ball should stay in play for several hits before the next player, E or F, becomes the net player. Players should rotate from the net position to the baseline position after about 5 minutes of play.

Coaching Points:

- Emphasize quick, explosive steps to move into position.
- Players at the net should watch the baseliner for clues as to whether he is planning to drive or lob and move accordingly.

DRILL **10.8**

Two Steps Up or Three Back

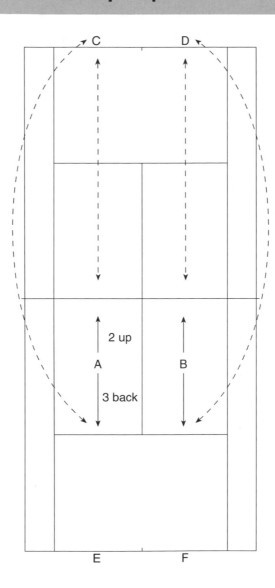

DRILL **10.9**

 4-Ball

Patterns

40 and 41

Category: *Net Play*

Purpose: To practice coming in to the net with an approach shot, followed by a volley, and ending the point with an overhead smash.

Equipment: Targets of towels or disks.

Level: Intermediate to professional.

Time: 15 to 20 minutes.

Procedure: Player B begins the play by hitting a short ball to player A, who hits an approach shot down the line and follows the ball to the net. Player B hits a passing shot down the line, which player A volleys crosscourt to the open court. Player B replies with a lob over player A's backhand side. Player A moves around the lob and hits a winning overhead smash crosscourt to target T_1. When the point is completed, players C and D replace players A and B.

Coaching Points:

- Encourage players to hit the ball at about three-quarter speed so that they can control the sequence of shots.
- If the lob is short, players have the option of angling it away or bouncing it over the fence.

DRILL **10.9**

4-Ball

Patterns

40 and 41

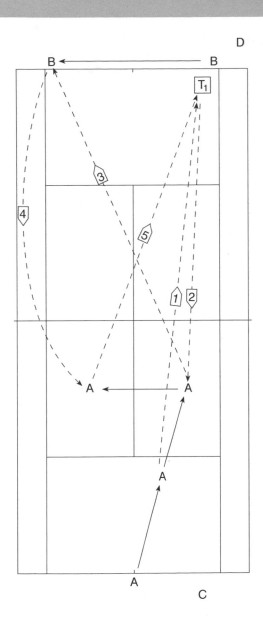

DRILL **10.10**

 ## Angles Away

Pattern

40

Category: *Net Play*

Purpose: To practice angling the overhead smash away off the court.

Equipment: Targets of hoops or cones.

Level: Beginner to advanced.

Time: 10 minutes.

Procedure: Players line up in a single-file line behind the service line. The coach hits a ball to player A, who takes it out of the air with a volley deep to target T_1. The coach either plays that ball or puts another ball in play by hitting a short lob. Player A smashes the ball, aiming for target T_2, then goes to the end of the line. Player B repeats the two-shot sequence, followed by players C and D. After 5 minutes, repeat the same pattern on the other half of the court.

Coaching Points:

- After the volley, players should close in as if to expect a passing shot. When they recognize the lob, the first move is to turn the shoulders sideways and back up as a football quarterback does when retreating to pass.
- The overhead smash should be contacted well in front of the body to angle it away.

DRILL **10.10**

Angles Away

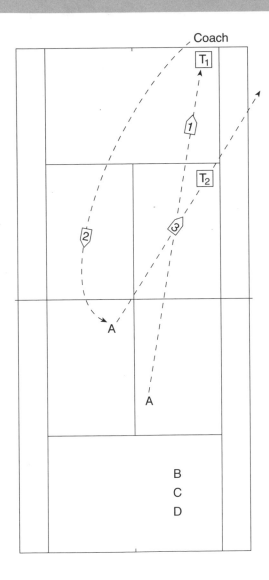

Coach

DRILL **10.11**

 Hammer the Smash

Pattern

40

Category: *Net Play*

Purpose: To practice smashing the ball over the fence.

Equipment: Targets of hoops or cones.

Level: Intermediate to professional.

Time: 10 minutes.

Procedure: Players line up in a single-file line behind the "T." The coach hits a ball to player A, who takes it out of the air with a volley deep to target T_1. Player A follows the volley and sprints up to touch the net with her racquet as the coach puts up a short lob. Player A recovers her balance by quickly moving back to get behind the ball and then smashes it hard so that the bounce will carry the ball up against or over the fence.

Player A returns to the end of the line, and player B takes a turn, followed by players C and D. If any player is successful in bouncing the ball over the fence, the next player in line must run around to retrieve the ball.

Coaching Points:

- This drill is a good opportunity to teach players the proper movement forward and backward at the net. Teach them to stay balanced, even while they explode aggressively to the ball.
- A full turn sideways and a pronounced wrist snap are key to projecting the ball down into the court so that the bounce will carry it over the fence.

DRILL **10.11**

Hammer the Smash

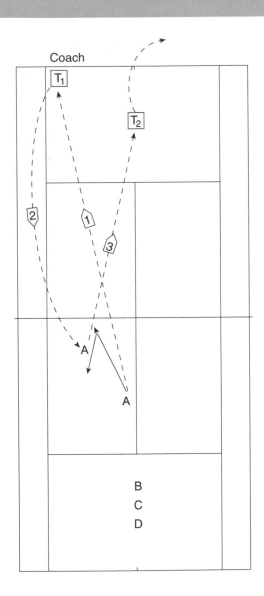

DRILL **10.12**

 Deep Overheads

Pattern

41

Category: *Net Play*

Purpose: To practice hitting overhead smashes from moderately deep lobs and moving in to the net to end the point with a volley.

Equipment: Targets of towels or hoops.

Level: Intermediate to professional.

Time: 20 minutes.

Procedure: Player A begins from the ideal volleying position halfway between the service line and the net. The coach puts the ball in play with a moderately deep lob that forces player A to retreat and use a scissors kick jump to smash the ball. The smash should be directed deep crosscourt to the target. Player C, who began the point from the middle of the baseline, moves across and tries to play the smash back down the line. Player A has recovered after the smash to close in to the net and should volley player C's return deep or short crosscourt to win the point. Players B and D repeat the pattern. After about 10 minutes, switch the drill to the other side of the court.

Coaching Points:

- Stress recovery after the overhead and readiness for the next shot.
- Urge the players defending against the smashes to "soften" their hands and take almost no backswing to compensate for the high speed of the oncoming ball.

Deep Overheads

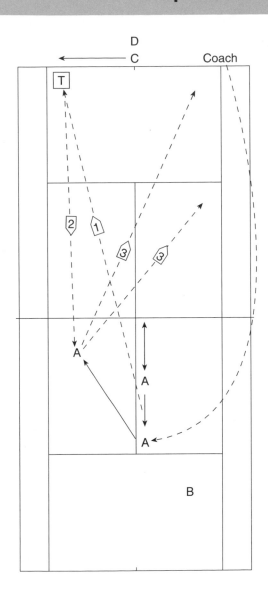

DRILL **10.13**

 Overhead From the Bounce

Pattern

42

Category: *Net Play*

Purpose: To practice hitting the overhead smash after the ball has bounced against a very high lob or those complicated by wind or sun. After the smash, players should practice closing in to the net to complete the point.

Equipment: None.

Level: Intermediate to professional.

Time: 15 to 20 minutes.

Procedure: Player A begins the drill by looping a heavy topspin shot deep to the backhand corner, forcing player B to retreat and play a high defensive lob. Player A positions himself behind the ball after the bounce and smashes it to the largest area of the court. Player A then follows the path of the ball to the net, expecting a return. Player B covers the shot and tries to pass player A at the net. The point is played to conclusion. Players A and B are then replaced in the drill by players C and D, who repeat the pattern.

Coaching Points:

- Players should apply some spin to the overhead smash and hit up on it, just as with the serve, because they are fairly deep in the court.
- As players move in to the net after the smash, remind them to split-step so that they can change direction to play the volley.

DRILL **10.13**

Overhead From the Bounce

Pattern

42

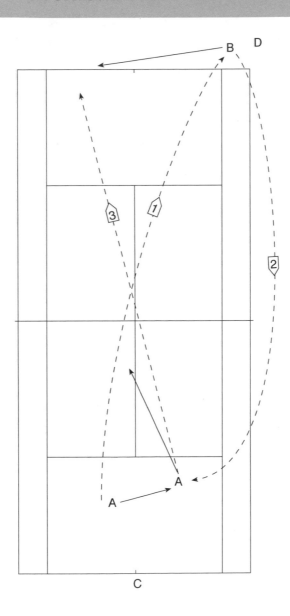

DRILL **10.14**

Lobs and Smashes

Patterns

40 - 42

Category: *Net Play*

Purpose: To practice the overhead smash and develop the touch and technique of defending against the smash.

Equipment: None.

Level: Beginner to advanced.

Time: 10 to 15 minutes.

Procedure: Player A tries to put away overhead smashes anywhere within the doubles court. Players B, C, and D defend by lofting defensive lobs and trying to return every smash. After 2 or 3 minutes, players rotate clockwise to a new position.

Coaching Points:

- Award a point each time the player hitting the overhead smash hits a ball that is not returned over the net. At the end of the drill, the player with the most points wins.
- Stress the importance of angling the overhead smash rather than trying to overpower the opponent with speed.

DRILL **10.14**

Lobs and Smashes

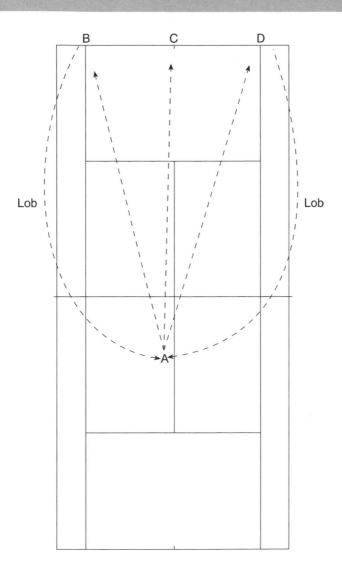

Patterns

40 - 42

 *PART V*

Defensive Patterns and Drills

Defensive play against a net player involves hitting the ball past her to the left or right or lobbing a shot over her head. Your choice of shots depends on your position in the court, your strengths and weaknesses, and how close your opponent is to the net.

Many of the drills in part IV can be used to practice your defensive shots while your partner works on her volleying skills. Add those drills to the ones in chapter 12 to complete your assortment of drill activities for defensive play.

Chapter 11

Defensive Patterns

Passing shots and lobs are the defensive weapons of tennis. The patterns in this chapter will show you how to groove your thinking to reverse the momentum of a point so that you will become the aggressor. Like the rest of the patterns in this book, the 15 patterns in this chapter are based on the principles of high-percentage tennis.

In most cases, you should think of passing as a two-shot sequence. First, get your opponent in trouble with a low shot. After a weak volley, pass him on the second shot. Many inexperienced players will panic when the opponent rushes the net and try to pass him by overhitting the attempt at a passing shot.

When hitting passing shots, aim lower to the net (about one to three feet) than on your normal groundstrokes. Use topspin on most passing shots to dip the ball at your opponent's feet or to keep the ball in the court on an offensive lob. Accelerate the racquet sharply upward to impart severe topspin.

If you are in trouble, on the dead run, or pushed deep in your backcourt, counter with a high defensive lob to the longest part of the court to allow time to recover. When the wind is in your face or the sun is in your opponent's eyes, the lob can be a most effective shot. If you are successful in forcing your opponent to retreat from the net position, look for an opportunity to sneak in yourself and surprise her.

You should choose a passing shot when your opponent does not close in to the net, her volley is undependable, the wind is at your back, or you can play the ball from inside your baseline. Choose to

lob when your opponent is close to the net, her smash is undependable, the sun is in her eyes, the wind is in your face, or you are forced
deep behind your baseline. Disguise your shots so that she cannot
anticipate whether you are going to drive or lob.

PATTERN **43**

Against a Deep Crosscourt Approach

Pass Down the Line

Objective: Although this requires changing the direction of the ball, your opponent will need to cover a lot of ground to cut off the shot.

Drills: 12.1, 12.2, 12.3

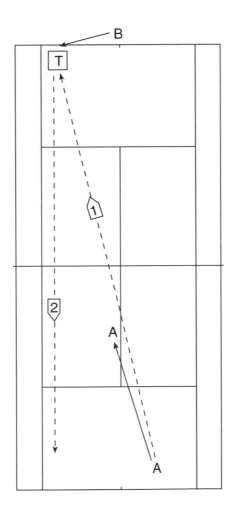

PATTERN **44**

Against a Deep Crosscourt Approach

Pass Crosscourt

Objective: Drive a low topspin passing shot back crosscourt. Hopefully you will be hitting the ball behind your opponent.

Drills: 12.1, 12.2, 12.3

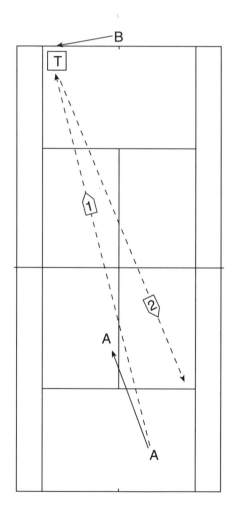

PATTERN **45**

Against a Moderate Down-the-Line Approach

Pass Crosscourt

Objective: Drive a low topspin passing shot crosscourt by taking the ball early and on the rise.

Drills: 12.1, 12.2, 12.4

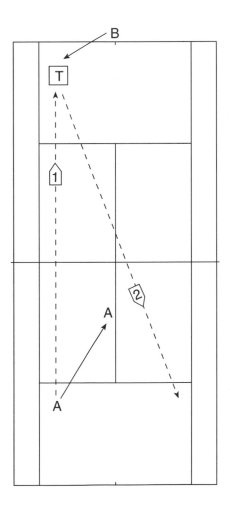

PATTERN 46

Against a Moderate Down-the-Line Approach

Use a Two-Shot Pass

Objective: On your first shot, hit a low and hard drive down the line to elicit a weak volley, and then hit the second passing shot crosscourt.

Drills: 12.1, 12.2, 12.4

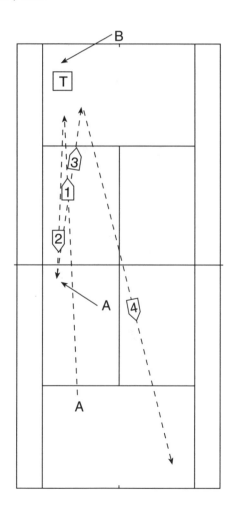

PATTERN **47**

Against an Approach up the Middle

Use a Two-Shot Pass

Objective: On your first shot, hit a forceful passing shot right at the net player to reduce the angles for a winning volley. On your next shot, look to hit a clear passing shot to either side.

Drill: 12.5

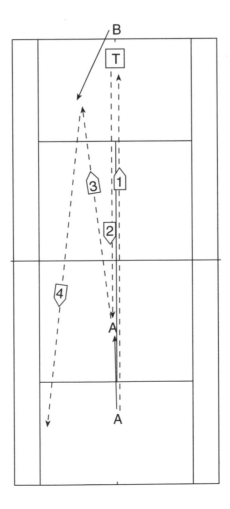

PATTERN **48**

Against an Approach up the Middle
Use a Two-Shot Pass Inside Out

Objective: On your first shot, hit a heavy topspin inside-out fore-hand so the ball dips below the net. Expect a volley down the line and hit your second passing shot sharply crosscourt.

Drill: 12.5

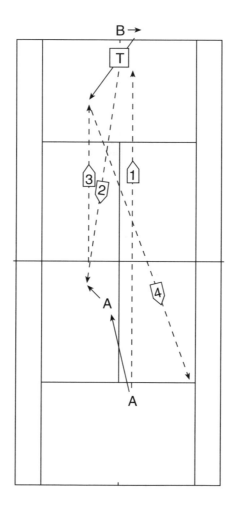

PATTERN **49**

Against a Weak Approach up the Middle

Overpower Your Opponent

Objective: If your opponent's approach shot lacks depth and pace, move around the ball to hit your strongest shot and "power" the ball crosscourt or down the line.

Drill: 12.6

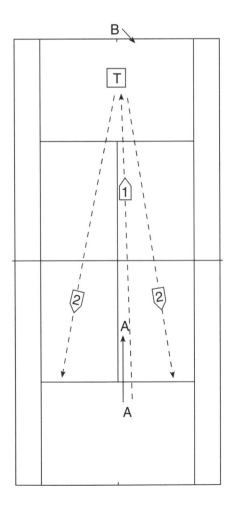

PATTERN **50**

Against a Deep Sliced Approach to Backhand
Use Two Shots to Pass, First Crosscourt, Then Down the Line

Objective: Get to the ball quickly and hit the high-percentage crosscourt pass to get your opponent in trouble. Expect a volley up the line and then pass on the second shot.

Drill: 12.7

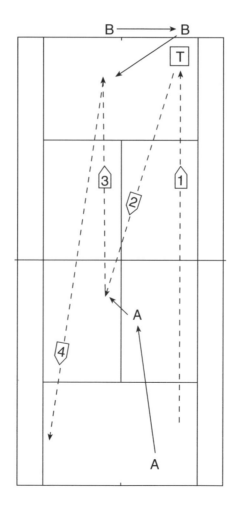

PATTERN **51**

Against a Deep Sliced Approach to Backhand

Use Two Shots to Pass, First Down the Line, Then Down the Opposite Line

Objective: Hit your first passing shot down the line and expect your opponent to volley crosscourt to the open court. Hit your second passing shot down the line on the other side of the court.

Drill: 12.8

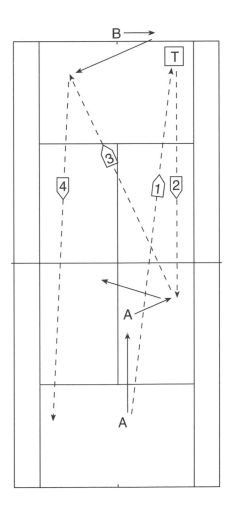

PATTERN **52**

Against a Deep Sliced Approach to Forehand

Use Two Shots to Pass

Objective: Get to the ball quickly and hit the high-percentage crosscourt pass to get your opponent in trouble. Expect a volley up the line and then pass on the second shot.

Drill: 12.7

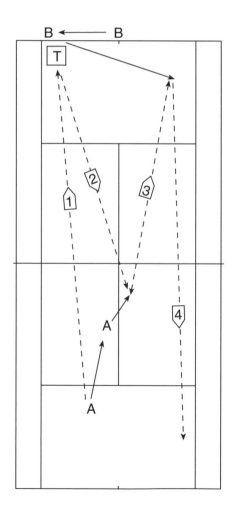

PATTERN **53**

Against a Deep Sliced Approach to Forehand

Use Two Shots to Pass, First Down the Line, Then Down the Opposite Line

Objective: Hit your first passing shot down the line and expect your opponent to volley crosscourt to the open court. Hit your second passing shot down the line on the other side of the court.

Drill: 12.8

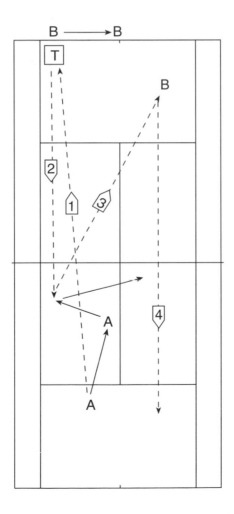

PATTERN **54**

Against a Short, Sliced Approach

Use a Two-Shot Pass

Objective: If the sliced approach is near the sideline to your back-hand and forces you to stretch to play the ball, hit a soft, low chip crosscourt on the first shot. Expect a weak volley and pass on the second shot.

Drill: 12.9

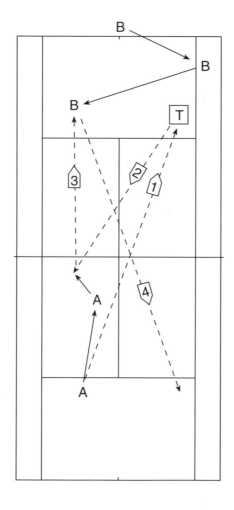

PATTERN **55**

Against a Short, Weak Volley
Drive at Opponent's Right Hip

Objective: After an aggressive drive at your opponent's right hip, expect a reflex volley, which you can then put away.

Drill: 12.10

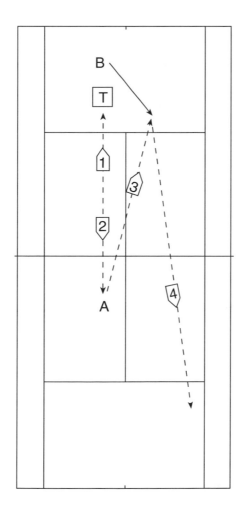

PATTERN **56**

Against an Approach to Your Backhand
Drive and Then Lob

Objective: After an approach, hit a passing shot low and down the line. If your opponent volleys to the open court, hit an offensive lob with heavy topspin over his backhand side.

Drill: 12.11

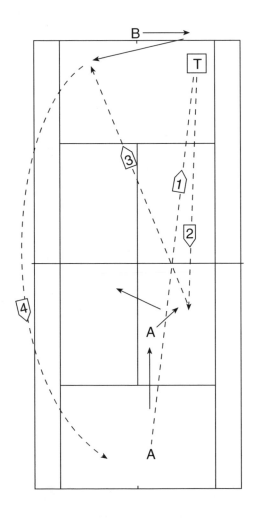

PATTERN 57

Against an Approach to Your Backhand

Drive and Then Lob Crosscourt

Objective: After an approach, hit a passing shot low and down the line. If your opponent volleys to the open court and closes in, hit an offensive lob with heavy topspin crosscourt to the longest part of the court.

Drill: 12.11

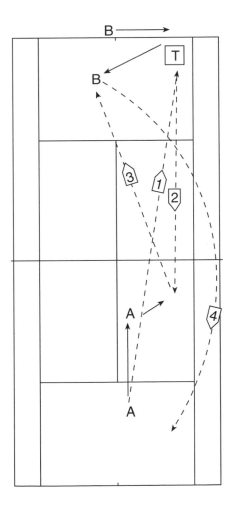

PATTERN **58**

Against a Deep Approach Shot

Hit a High Defensive Lob

Objective: If your opponent's approach pushes you very deep or pulls you wide off the court, hit a defensive lob to the largest court area to give yourself time to recover.

Drill: 12.12

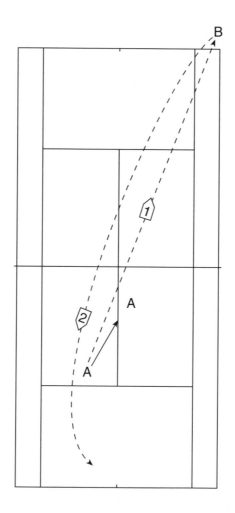

 **Chapter 12**

Defensive Drills

Michael Chang and Arantxa Sanchez-Vicario are masters of defensive play and have used their ability to neutralize attacking players in winning world championships. Patience and percentages are key factors in their success. You'll notice that many of the drills in this chapter require you to make several shots to win the point. Through these 12 drills, you too can develop patience when you are on the defensive.

DRILL **12.1**

Perfect 10

Patterns

43 - 46

Category: *Defensive Play*

Purpose: To learn to adjust the height and depth of groundstrokes for effective passing shots.

Equipment: A rope three feet above the net.

Level: Beginner to intermediate.

Time: 10 to 15 minutes.

Procedure: The coach feeds the players four balls in succession, which they try to hit in sequence to the following locations: deep crosscourt, short crosscourt, deep down the line, and short down the line. Each successful shot earns the point value shown, and hitting all four shots correctly earns a perfect 10. After their turn, players retrieve the four balls they hit and replace them in the hopper.

After a few minutes, players should switch to the backhand side, and as they gain some success, the coach can mix up the feeds to either side.

Coaching Points:

- Emphasize hitting the ball lower to the net than on normal groundstrokes and applying sufficient topspin for the ball to drop after it passes the net.
- Modify the drill to stress accuracy by adding targets.

DRILL **12.1**

Perfect 10

Patterns

43 - 46

1 pt   3 pts

Coach

2 pts   4 pts

3

1

2   4

Rope 3 feet above net

A

B C D

DRILL **12.2**

Passing Shot Warm-Up

Patterns

43 - 46

Category: *Defensive Play*

Purpose: To get the feel of hitting passing shots crosscourt and down the line during a warm-up session.

Equipment: None.

Level: Beginner to advanced.

Time: 10 to 15 minutes.

Procedure: Players A and B put the ball in play from the service line and stay there for the returning shot. Players C and D try to hit a topspin passing shot aimed at the short crosscourt angle, low to the net, and the point is played out. Players A and D work together at the same time as players B and C are performing the drill on the other side of the court. After a few minutes, players should rotate clockwise to the next position until they have practiced from each of the four locations.

Coaching Points:

- Although players A and B are in the unnatural position of remaining at the service line instead of closing in to the net, they will get good practice at digging out low volleys and half-volleys.
- For variation, players can hit the passing shot straight ahead rather than crosscourt.

DRILL **12.2**

Passing Shot Warm-Up

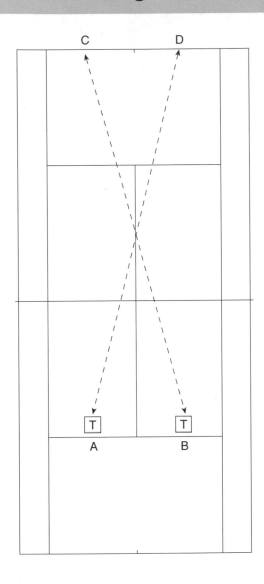

Patterns

43 - 46

DRILL **12.3**

One-Shot Pass—From Deep Approach Crosscourt

Patterns

43 and 44

Category: *Defensive Play*

Purpose: To defend against a deep crosscourt approach shot by hitting the passing shot either sharply crosscourt or down the line.

Equipment: None.

Level: Intermediate to professional.

Time: 20 minutes.

Procedure: Players A and B rally for four to six shots until player A gets a short ball. She then hits a deep crosscourt approach shot, which player B returns with a sharp angled crosscourt passing shot. Players C and D repeat the same pattern.

After 10 trials of this pattern for each pair, the passing shot should be hit down the line. After 10 more trials, allow the defender to choose either crosscourt or down the line.

When players have completed this sequence, go through the same progression of shots on the other side of the court.

Coaching Points:

- Point out that the crosscourt shot is very effective on clay or grass courts.
- If players are slow to close in or don't cover the line very well, the down-the-line shot is most effective.

DRILL **12.3**

One-Shot Pass—From Deep Approach Crosscourt

Patterns

43 and 44

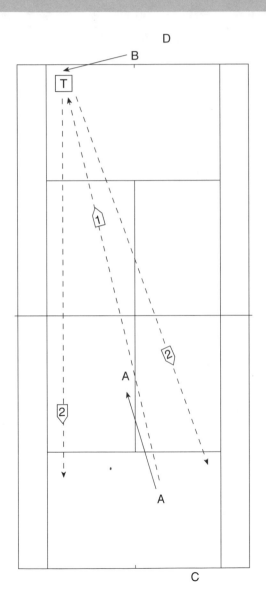

DRILL **12.4**

One-Shot Pass—From Moderate Down-the-Line Approach

Patterns

45 and 46

Category: *Defensive Play*

Purpose: To defend against a down-the-line approach shot with moderate depth by passing crosscourt or down the line.

Equipment: None.

Level: Intermediate to professional.

Time: 20 minutes.

Procedure: Players A and B rally for four to six shots until player A gets a short ball. He then hits a moderately deep approach shot down the line, which player B returns with a sharp angled crosscourt passing shot. Players C and D repeat the same pattern.

After 10 trials of this pattern for each pair, the passing shot should be hit down the line. After 10 more trials, allow the defender to choose either crosscourt or down the line. Repeat the drill on the other side of the court.

To add an element of competition, players A and C can compete against players B and D by earning points each time they win the play.

Coaching Points:

- Be sure that players close in as they normally would after the approach shot so the defensive player is faced with a realistic situation.
- Be sure to rotate all of the players to the defensive position during the time allotted.

DRILL **12.4**

One-Shot Pass—From Moderate Down-the-Line Approach

Patterns

45 and 46

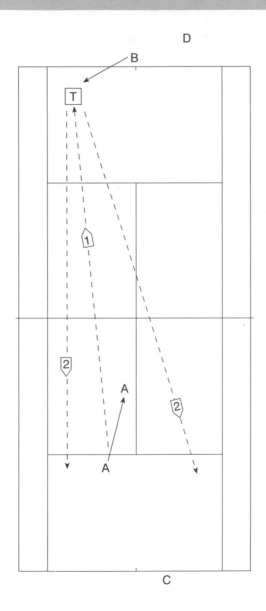

DRILL **12.5**

 ## Two-Shot Pass—Navel Attack

Patterns

47 and 48

Category: *Defensive Play*

Purpose: To defend against an approach shot deep down the middle of the court with a two-shot sequence to pass.

Equipment: None.

Level: Intermediate to professional.

Time: 10 to 15 minutes.

Procedure: Players A and C rally until player A gets a short ball and hits a deep approach shot up the middle. Player C drives her first passing shot hard right at player A. Because of the speed of the ball, player A is likely to play a weak defensive volley; player C can then hit an easy passing shot, either crosscourt or down the line. Players B and D repeat the pattern.

Coaching Points:

- This drill teaches players to be patient with the first passing shot when they are deep and have no angles available.
- The hard drive right at the net player is particularly effective against players who have trouble getting out of the way of a ball.

DRILL **12.5**

Two-Shot Pass—Navel Attack

Patterns

47 and 48

DRILL **12.6**

 Inside-Out or Hook Forehand Pass

Pattern

49

Category: *Defensive Play*

Purpose: To defend against an approach shot deep down the middle of the court with an inside-out forehand or hook forehand.

Equipment: None.

Level: Intermediate to professional.

Time: 10 to 15 minutes.

Procedure: Players A and C rally until player A gets a short ball and hits a deep approach shot up the middle. Player C quickly steps around the ball and hits either an inside-out forehand drive crosscourt or hooks the ball sharply down the sideline. Player A tries to play a volley, and the point continues until conclusion. Players B and D step in and repeat the pattern. Add together points earned by players A and B and those earned by players C and D. When one team has scored 11 points, switch the attacking and defending roles.

Coaching Points:

- The passing shot should be well disguised so that the net player cannot anticipate the direction.
- The inside-out forehand requires quick footwork to move around into position.

DRILL **12.6**

Inside-Out or Hook Forehand Pass

Pattern

49

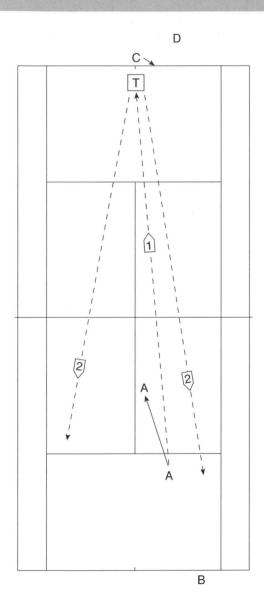

DRILL **12.7**

 Two-Shot Pass—Crosscourt First

Patterns

50 and 52

Category: *Defensive Play*

Purpose: To defend against a deep slice approach shot down the line with a two-shot sequence beginning with the crosscourt shot.

Equipment: None.

Level: Intermediate to professional.

Time: 20 minutes.

Procedure: Players A and C rally for four to six balls until player A gets a short ball and hits a deep sliced approach shot down the line. Player C hits the first passing shot crosscourt low with topspin and anticipates a weak volley by player A to the open court. Player C then steps in and hits a winning passing shot down the line. Next, players B and D repeat the pattern.

After all players have had a turn in the defensive position, repeat the pattern on the other side of the court.

Coaching Points:

- The key to success in this pattern is hitting with topspin to make the crosscourt shot dip low as it passes over the net and forcing the opponent to volley up.
- Point out that this is a very effective pattern on a slow court surface such as clay.

Two-Shot Pass—Crosscourt First

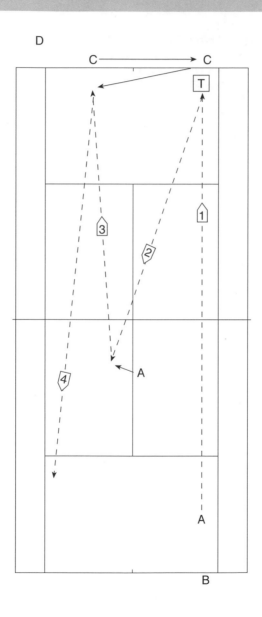

DRILL **12.8**

Two-Shot Pass—Down the Line First

Patterns

51 and 53

Category: *Defensive Play*

Purpose: To defend against a deep slice approach shot down the line with a two-shot sequence beginning with the down-the-line pass.

Equipment: None.

Level: Intermediate to professional.

Time: 20 minutes.

Procedure: Players A and C rally for four to six balls until player A gets a short ball and hits a deep sliced approach shot down the line. Player C hits the first passing shot low down the line and anticipates a volley by player A to the open court. Player C then steps in and hits a winning passing shot down the opposite sideline. Next, players B and D repeat the pattern.

After all players have had a turn in the defensive position, repeat the same pattern on the other side of the court. As a variation, allow the defensive players to choose whether to hit the crosscourt or down-the-line shot first in their two-shot sequence.

Coaching Points:

- The defensive player must get to the ball early and keep the down-the-line shot low to the net to prevent the net player from hitting a winning volley.
- Point out that this is a very effective pattern on a slow court surface such as clay.

DRILL **12.8**

Two-Shot Pass—Down the Line First

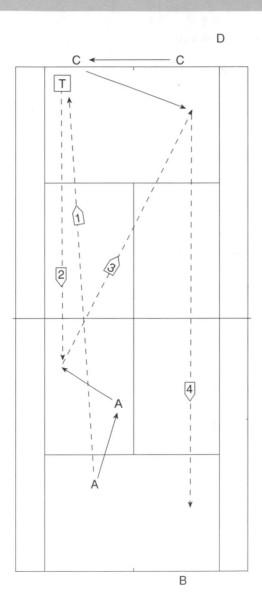

Patterns

51 and 53

DRILL **12.9**

 ## Two-Shot Pass—Crosscourt Chip First

Pattern

54

Category: *Defensive Play*

Purpose: To defend against a short sliced approach shot that causes you to stretch. Use a two-shot passing sequence beginning with a crosscourt chip.

Equipment: None.

Level: Intermediate to professional.

Time: 10 to 15 minutes.

Procedure: Players A and C rally backhands crosscourt until player A gets a short, wide ball. Player A slices a short angled approach shot and follows the ball to the net. Player C plays a soft, low crosscourt chip and anticipates a weak volley down the line from player A, who has to reverse direction. Player C runs over and hits a winning passing shot crosscourt. Players B and D step in to repeat the pattern.

Coaching Points:
- This pattern is typically hit backhand to backhand as players are more likely to slice the ball on that side.
- Because the angle is so severe, players must hit the chip crosscourt at a moderate pace, since a ball that is struck sharply is likely to go wide.

DRILL **12.9**

Two-Shot Pass—Crosscourt Chip First

Pattern

54

DRILL **12.10**

Make Him Pay

Pattern

55

Category: *Defensive Play*

Purpose: To make opponent pay the price for hitting a short volley that sits up by hitting the passing shot right at him.

Equipment: None.

Level: Intermediate to professional.

Time: 10 minutes.

Procedure: Player A puts the ball in play from the service line and moves in to the net. Player D hits an aggressive drive at player A's right hip and expects a weak volley that sits up for the passing shot. Players B and C repeat the sequence.

Coaching Points:

- Point out that this shot is often effective against a serve-and-volleyer because they anticipate passing shots well if you try to pass on either side.
- Urge players to be ready for anything after the shot at the opponent's right hip, because there is likely to be a reflex or mis-hit volley that surprises them.

DRILL **12.10**

Make Him Pay

DRILL **12.11**

 Lob Your Second Shot

Patterns

56 and 57

Category: *Defensive Play*

Purpose: To defend against the approach by hitting the first passing shot low and an offensive lob on the second shot against a player who closes in.

Equipment: None.

Level: Intermediate to professional.

Time: 20 minutes.

Procedure: Players A and C rally for four to six shots until player A gets a short ball. Player A hits an approach shot down the line and follows it to the net. Player C hits the first passing shot at player A's feet, and player A volleys or half-volleys to the open court. Player C then hits an offensive lob with heavy topspin over player A's backhand side or crosscourt to the longest part of the court. Players B and D step in and repeat the pattern.

After all players have had the opportunity to play the defender's role, switch the drill to the other side of the court. Depending on the level of skill, players may be allowed to complete the point after the lob.

Coaching Points:

- For the offensive lob, players must get to the ball quickly and impart heavy topspin by accelerating the racquet sharply upward.
- Stress disguising the lob so that the net player cannot anticipate it.

DRILL **12.11**

Lob Your Second Shot

Patterns

56 and 57

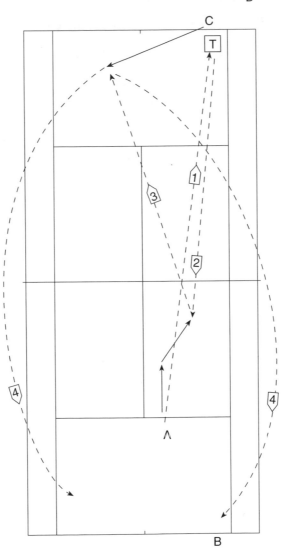

DRILL **12.12**

 Two Balls Across, One Wide

Pattern

58

Category: *Defensive Play*

Purpose: To practice the high defensive lob.

Equipment: Target of hoops, cones, or disks.

Level: Beginner to advanced.

Time: 10 minutes.

Procedure: All players line up on one side of the court and move across the baseline as the coach feeds two balls in succession across the baseline. Players drive the first two balls to target T_1, and then the coach hits the third ball behind them. Players must turn and sprint to the ball and hit a high defensive lob to target T_2. After 5 minutes, switch the drill to the other side of the court so that the lob is hit with the forehand.

Coaching Points:

- The lob should be hit high enough to allow players to recover to the center of the court.
- Encourage players to apply a little underspin as they slide under the ball to control the depth of the lob. The follow-through should be long and in an upward direction.

Two Balls Across, One Wide

Pattern

58

Pattern Finder

BACKCOURT PATTERNS *(cont.)*

Return of Serve Patterns *(cont.)*

Pattern	Page	Drills
#14 Against a Short, Weak Serve; Hit a Forcing Shot Down the Line	35	4.10, 4.11, 4.12
#15 Against a Short, Weak Serve; Hit a Forcing Shot Crosscourt	36	4.10, 4.11
#16 Against a Short, Weak Serve; Chip or Drive Down the Line and Come to the Net	37	4.12
#17 Against a Serve-and-Volleyer; Return Low at the Server's Feet	38	4.13
#18 Against a Serve-and-Volleyer; Return Down the Line	39	4.13

Groundstroke Patterns

Pattern	Page	Drills
#19 Rally Crosscourt; Attack a Short Ball Down the Line	70	6.1, 6.2, 6.3, 6.4, 6.5, 6.6
#20 Rally Crosscourt; Attack a Short Ball Crosscourt	71	6.1, 6.3, 6.5, 6.6
#21 Rally Crosscourt to Get Short, Wide Ball; Hit a Severe Angle	72	6.1, 6.3, 6.5, 6.7
#22 From a Ball Down the Middle; Drive Inside-Out Through the Court	73	6.5, 6.8, 6.9
#23 From a Ball in Left Half of Court; Drive Inside-Out Off the Court	74	6.5, 6.8
#24 When Driven Deep; Hit Looping Drives to Opponent's Backhand	75	6.5, 6.10
#25 Exchange Sliced Backhands; Attack a Short Ball	76	6.5, 6.12
#26 Against Deep Shots in the Middle; Hit High and Deep Down the Middle	77	6.5, 6.11

MIDCOURT PATTERNS

	Pattern	Page	Drills
#27	If Ball Is Above the Net; Drive Hard and Flat Down the Line	109	8.1, 8.2, 8.5, 8.9, 8.10, 8.11
#28	If Ball Is Above the Net; Drive Crosscourt for a Winner	110	8.10, 8.11
#29	If Ball Is Below the Net; Slice Down the Line	111	8.1, 8.2, 8.3, 8.5, 8.9, 8.10, 8.11
#30	If Ball Is Below the Net; Drop Shot Down the Line	112	8.4, 8.10, 8.11
#31	From a Ball in the Middle; Approach Down the Middle	113	8.6, 8.10, 8.11
#32	From a Ball in the Middle; Use an Inside-Out Forehand Approach	114	8.7, 8.10, 8.11
#33	From a Deep, High-Bouncing Shot; Use a Looping Topspin Approach	115	8.8, 8.10, 8.11
#34	From a Looped Shot; Move In and Hit an Approach Volley	116	8.12

NET PLAY PATTERNS

	Pattern	Page	Drills
#35	If Ball Is Above the Net; Volley to Opponent's Weakness	147	10.1, 10.2, 10.5
#36	If Ball Is Below the Net; Volley Deep Down the Line	148	10.1, 10.2, 10.3
#37	After Your Approach, if Ball Is Above the Net; Volley Deep Crosscourt	149	10.1, 10.2, 10.4
#38	Serve Wide and Volley to the Open Court	150	10.1, 10.6
#39	Serve to the "T" and Volley Behind Opponent or to a Weakness	151	10.1, 10.7
#40	If Lob Is Short; Angle Your Overhead Away	152	10.8, 10.9, 10.10, 10.11, 10.14
#41	If Lob Is Deep; Aim Your Overhead Crosscourt	153	10.9, 10.12, 10.14
#42	On High Lobs; Let Ball Bounce and Aim Crosscourt	154	10.13, 10.14

DEFENSIVE PLAY PATTERNS

	Pattern	Page	Drills
#43	Against a Deep Crosscourt Approach; Pass Down the Line	189	12.1, 12.2, 12.3
#44	Against a Deep Crosscourt Approach; Pass Crosscourt	190	12.1, 12.2, 12.3
#45	Against a Moderate Down-the-Line Approach; Pass Crosscourt	191	12.1, 12.2, 12.4
#46	Against a Moderate Down the Line Approach; Use a Two-Shot Pass	192	12.1, 12.2, 12.4
#47	Against an Approach up the Middle; Use a Two-Shot Pass	193	12.5
#48	Against an Approach up the Middle; Use a Two-Shot Pass Inside Out	194	12.5
#49	Against a Weak Approach up the Middle; Overpower Your Opponent	195	12.6
#50	Against a Deep Sliced Approach to Backhand; Use Two Shots to Pass; First Crosscourt, Then Down the Line.	196	12.7
#51	Against a Deep Sliced Approach to Backhand; Use Two Shots to Pass; First Down the Line, Then Down the Opposite Line	197	12.8
#52	Against a Deep Sliced Approach to Forehand; Use Two Shots to Pass	198	12.7
#53	Against a Deep Sliced Approach to Forehand; Use Two Shots to Pass; First Down the Line, Then Down the Opposite Line	199	12.8
#54	Against a Short, Sliced Approach; Use a Two-Shot Pass	200	12.9
#55	Against a Short, Weak Volley; Drive at Opponent's Right Hip	201	12.10
#56	Against an Approach to Your Backhand; Drive and Then Lob	202	12.11
#57	Against an Approach to Your Backhand; Drive and Then Lob Crosscourt	203	12.11
#58	Against a Deep Approach Shot, Hit a High Defensive Lob	204	12.12

About the Author

The United States Tennis Association (USTA) is the governing body for tennis in the United States. Its mission is to promote and develop the growth of tennis. The USTA's membership includes more than 500,000 individuals and nearly 6,500 organizations, including schools, park and recreation departments, community tennis associations, and tennis clubs.

The USTA is widely known as the owner and operator of the U.S. Open Championships, one of the four Grand Slam tournaments in worldwide tennis competition. It also sponsors amateur tennis competition for players of all ages and abilities. More than 5 million schoolchildren are introduced to tennis each year through USTA school programs, and opportunities for further instruction and play are provided by a menu of USTA entry-level programs.

A full range of player development and sport-science programs is offered at Player Development Headquarters in Key Biscayne, Florida, at 120 Area Training Centers throughout the country, and in communities (through a network of Local Excellence Training Programs). In addition, the USTA emphasizes coaching education and development through an ambitious offering of coaching seminars, workshops, and conferences. It works closely with the two major organizations certifying coaches—the U.S. Professional Tennis Association (USPTA) and the U.S. Professional Tennis Registry (USPTR)—together accounting for more than 18,000 members.

Ron Woods, director of player development for the USTA, wrote *Tennis Tactics* with the help of the USTA sport-science staff and coaches. Ron is responsible for planning and implementing programs that help players—from beginners to veterans in the professional ranks—achieve their maximum potential.

Ron also is a senior staff member for the USTA committees in charge of player development, sport science, Olympic tennis, junior competition, and collegiate tennis. A former member of the International Tennis Federation's Coaches Commission, he serves on the coaching committee of the U.S. Olympic Committee. The USPTA honored him as 1982 National Coach of the Year and designated him a Master Professional in 1984. Ron is also an honorary member of the USPTR.